Preserves
& Pickles

Preserves & Pickles

Alison Burt

Octopus Books

First published 1973 by
Octopus Books Limited
59 Grosvenor Street, London W1

ISBN 0 7064 0272 3

© 1973 Octopus Books Limited

Distributed in Australia by
Rigby Limited
30 North Terrace, Kent Town
Adelaide, South Australia 5067

Produced by Mandarin Publishers Limited
14 Westlands Road, Quarry Bay, Hong Kong

Printed in Hong Kong

Contents

Weights and Measures 7

Introduction 8

Jams, Jellies and Marmalades 11

Fruit Butters and Curds 58

Fruit Drinks 64

Brandied and Candied Fruit 67

Vinegars 72

Pickles 74

Chutneys, Sauces and Ketchups 85

Bottling Fruit and Vegetables 99

Freezing Fruit and Vegetables 115

Drying Fruit, Vegetables and Herbs 120

Salting Vegetables and Curing Hams and Bacon .. 124

Index 126

Acknowledgments 128

Weights and Measures

All the measures used in this book are based on Imperial weights and measures. The only differences between the Imperial and American weights are the pint measure and the tablespoon. The American measure, where vital, is given in brackets after the Imperial measure in the recipes. Frequently, a housewife is without scales; for this eventuality, a cup measurement is given wherever possible. It must be understood however that sugar and salt, which are two of the most important ingredients in the recipes, take up different cup measurements according to how refined they are. The salt used in the cup measurements refers to refined cooking salt NOT table salt or block salt which has been scraped at home. The white sugar used in the cup measurements refers to granulated sugar NOT castor (superfine), preserving or lump sugar unless specifically stated. THIS IS IMPORTANT TO MAINTAIN THE CORRECT RECIPE BALANCE. Use scales whenever possible for complete accuracy.

Imperial	*American*
1 pint (20 fl. oz.)	$2\frac{1}{2}$ cups
$\frac{1}{2}$ pint (10 fl. oz.)	$1\frac{1}{4}$ cups
$\frac{1}{4}$ pint (5 fl. oz.)	$\frac{5}{8}$ cup
8 fl. oz.	1 cup
1 tablespoon (20 ml.)	$1\frac{1}{4}$ tablespoons
1 teaspoon (5 ml.)	1 teaspoon

All the spoon measurements in this book are LEVEL.

Introduction

Making your own preserves is a fascinating and satisfying occupation. The whole object of preserving is to be able to keep food for a long time; in the case of fruit and vegetables, from one season to the next. Whether you grow all your own produce or simply buy lots of fresh fruit and vegetables in season, you will find that home preserving is an economical proposition.

All produce to be preserved must be in first-class condition and should be processed as soon as possible after gathering. If you grow your own, this is no problem but if you are buying from the greengrocer or farmer, do be careful and select only the best. Some farmers will allow you to pick your own fruit and vegetables, some even prefer it.

Fruit and vegetables which are picked and preserved on the same day will have the best flavour. This is one discovery you will make about home preserved produce—the flavours are by far superior to anything you can buy in the shops— and they can be varied to suit your own individual likes and dislikes.

The methods of preserving in this book are all designed to keep the food in its prime condition without the addition of any special chemical preservative. It could be argued that sugar, vinegar and salt are used as chemicals for preserving but these ingredients have become accepted as part of the essential flavour of preserves and they are all readily available in shops and supermarkets.

Heating, freezing and drying are other methods of preserving. All the different methods mentioned make delicious preserves but the instructions must be followed carefully for successful results. It is a good idea to read through the introduction to the chapter before starting a recipe, to help prevent any expensive mistakes. If you are in doubt as to whether your family will like any particular preserve, make just a small "test" quantity first.

All the recipes given can be divided in half or doubled, but it might be necessary to adjust the amount of water or vinegar used when making jam or chutney. The more preserves you make, the more enthusiastic you will become, because the results are so rewarding. You will come to know which varieties of fruit and vegetables are best for which method of preserving. If you are faced with an extremely large amount of one fruit or vegetable, look at the index to see the different ways in which it can be preserved, rather than make a huge supply of one preserve. For instance, apples can be made into jam, jelly, apple butter or cheese, but can also be made into chutney, can be bottled, dried and frozen; plums make good jam but can also be turned into chutney or even pickled whole.

Some fruit, vegetables and nuts can be stored in a cool place rather than being preserved. This storage time is limited but if you have the space, it is worth it for keeping whole, perfect, fresh produce. The ideal store room is cool, moist and dark. Warm, dry atmospheres make the fruit and vegetables shrivel and dry up.

Spread the produce on to trays or racks in a single layer so that the individual fruit, vegetables and nuts are not touching each other. Inspect them at intervals, turning them over to help prevent mould in vegetables or mildew in nuts. The produce must be mature and at peak condition; make sure that onions and nuts are thoroughly dry before being put in store and do not shell the nuts. Take precautions against mice or rats getting to the produce.

Apples, pears and root vegetables are most suitable for this method of storage; do not attempt to keep soft fruits or green vegetables by this method.

Jams, Jellies and Marmalades

Jams, jellies and marmalades are all basically the same type of preserve. They are all made from cooked fruits, have sugar added and depend, for a good set, on pectin and acid being present in the correct quantities.

Choosing the Fruit

Practically every fruit can be made into jam, jelly or marmalade to make a delicious preserve. If you can, use slightly under-ripe fruit. The preparation of each fruit is given with each individual recipe but bear in mind that the flavour of the preserve will only be as good as the ingredients used, so select the fruit carefully and discard any bad parts.

Cooking the Fruit

First you must choose the cooking pan. This can be stainless steel, aluminium or unchipped enamel coated. Copper pans should only be used for gooseberry jam, as they tend to destroy vitamins, but give a good green colour to jam. Choose a wide pan so that the liquid can be reduced quickly by boiling. The pan should never be more than two-thirds full at any time so make sure it is big enough for the amount of jam you intend to make.

The first stage of making jam, jelly or marmalade is to place the prepared fruit in the cooking pan, add water if necessary and cook gently until the fruit has softened. The time will vary according to the fruit used.

It is this cooking which extracts the pectin from the fruit. If the recipe calls for extra acid (e.g. lemon juice) to be added, to help this process, put it in the pan with the fruit at the beginning of the cooking time.

Straining the Fruit for Jelly

If the fruit is being made into jelly, it is at this point that it should be strained. For a clear bright jelly, it is important to obtain as clear a fruit juice as possible. It is preferable to use a specially made jelly bag, but this is not absolutely necessary; 3–4 thicknesses of muslin or a double thickness of clean tea towel will work just as well, but are more trouble to use!

Buy a jelly bag if you intend to make a lot of jelly. Scald the jelly bag by pouring boiling water through it then place the fruit pulp in the bag and allow the juice to drip through unaided into a clean bowl. This may take a fair time, but if the bag is squeezed or the pulp pressed in any way, the juice may be cloudy. If the fruit is rich in pectin (see below), the pulp can be returned to the saucepan after 10–15 minutes' straining, with more water (about half the amount originally used). Bring to the boil again for 30 minutes then strain the pulp again. The pulp may be left to drain overnight but in this case make the jelly as soon as possible the next day.

Pectin

Pectin is an almost flavourless substance which is found in most fruit although some fruits contain a lot more than others. It is essential to have the correct amount of pectin in jams, jellies and marmalades to ensure a good set.

Fruits which are high in pectin are: tart green cooking apples, crab apples, currants, green gooseberries, lemons, limes and bitter oranges.

Fruits which contain a moderate amount of pectin are: dessert apples, cranberries, damsons, grapes, loganberries and quinces.

Fruits which are low in pectin are: bananas, bilberries, blackberries, tart acid red cherries, under-ripe figs, japonica, melons, mulberries, plums, greengages and raspberries.

Fruits which contain very little or no pectin are: ripe apricots, sweet ripe cherries, elderberries, ripe figs, nectarines, peaches, pears, pineapple, ripe raspberries, rhubarb and strawberries.

If you are unsure as to whether the jam you are making contains sufficient pectin (or, in the case of jellies, sufficient to make a second extraction as described above) it is possible to test the cooked fruit pulp or juice.

To test for pectin: Place 1 teaspoon of fruit in a cup, add 3 teaspoons of methylated spirits and leave for 1 minute. At the end of this time a clot will have formed. If the clot is firm, there is plenty of pectin; a softer clot which breaks easily into smaller clots indicates only a moderate

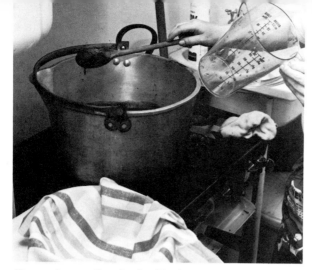

Preparing to Strain the Fruit

Straining the Fruit

amount of pectin; a very soft clot which breaks into many smaller clots even when the cup is moved, means that the pectin content is poor.

There are 4 ways in which pectin can be added to jams and jellies. Citrus fruits are rarely low in pectin and the pectin test need not be carried out when making marmalade.

One way to supplement pectin is to use commercial pectin. This is available in liquid or powder form and the manufacturer's instructions should be carefully followed. Another way is to combine two fruits in one jam or jelly, one low in pectin, the other high. The classic combination is blackberry and apple. Or you can use fruit juice that is high in pectin (like apple or redcurrant) in place of some of the water. Finally, the rinds of citrus fruits are rich in pectin and you can add pectin by tying the rinds in a muslin bag and putting this in the pan with the fruit while it is cooking. If you use too much citrus fruit, however, it will affect the flavour of the fruit you are cooking.

Adding the Sugar

When the fruit is cooked, the juice strained (for jelly) and the pectin content checked, then you can add the sugar. Weigh the sugar carefully, using preserving or lump sugar for preference; granulated sugar can also be successfully used but makes more scum. The cup measurements given in the recipes are for granulated sugar as this is the most economical and most readily available. Warm the sugar by placing it on a plate in a warm oven for a short time before adding it to boiling jam or marmalade. The strained juice for jelly-making will be cold; add the sugar cold and bring it slowly to the boil, then the jelly will have a richer colour. Stir the jam, jelly or marmalade until the sugar is dissolved and then boil rapidly until setting point is reached. Sugar toughens the skins of fruit so it is essential that this boiling is rapid. The colour and flavour of the jam, jelly or marmalade will also be affected by long boiling with the sugar.

Adding Sugar to Strawberries for Making Jam (right)
Pouring Strawberry Jam into Jars (far right)

To Test for Setting Point

There are 5 methods of testing to see if the jam, jelly or marmalade is at setting point and ready to be put into jars. To be absolutely sure, use 2 of the tests—for instance, a volume, weight or temperature test in conjunction with a flake or wrinkle test.

Volume test: The expected yield from each recipe is given. Fill as many one-pound jam jars as you will need with cold water. Tip the water into the cooking pan. Hold a wooden spoon handle upright in the centre of the pan and mark the level of the water. Throw the water away then make the jam as given in the recipe. When setting point is near, draw the pan off the heat and allow the bubbles to settle. Stand the spoon handle upright in the centre of the pan again. If the level of the jam is level with the mark on the spoon, setting point should have been reached. NOTE: This method can not be used when making jelly.

Weight Test: Weigh the empty cooking pan and the spoon. Make the jam as given in the recipe. When setting point is near, weigh the pan, spoon and jam again. If the setting point is reached the combined weight will be that as given for the yield, plus the weight of the clean pan and spoon as noted before.

Strawberry Jam

Strawberry Jam

NOTE: This method can not be used when making jelly.

Temperature Test: A sugar thermometer is ideal for this test. Place the thermometer in a jug of hot water. When the setting point is near, stir the jam and place the thermometer in the centre of the pan but not touching the bottom. The temperature should read 220–222°F (104–106°C) if setting point has been reached.

Flake Test: When you think that the setting point of the jam, jelly or marmalade has been reached, dip the wooden spoon into the pan and spoon up about one teaspoonful of the mixture. Holding the spoon over the pan, allow the hot preserve to cool slightly. If setting point has been reached, the jam, jelly or marmalade will not run off the spoon but will drop off cleanly in clots or "flakes".

Wrinkle Test: Spoon about one teaspoonful of the preserve onto a cold plate and put aside in a cold place for a few minutes. If setting point has been reached, the surface will have set and will wrinkle when pushed gently with the finger.

NOTE: Remove the cooking pan from the heat while doing this test as it takes a little time to cool and the jam, jelly or marmalade may become overcooked in the meantime.

Completing the Jam

When you know that setting point has been reached, remove the pan from the heat *immediately*. Allow the bubbles to subside, then skim. You should only remove the scum this once, at the end of the cooking time, or it is very wasteful. Scum can be reduced to a minimum if ¼ oz. butter is melted in the cooking pan before cooking is started.

Have ready the required number of jars, very clean and warmed. Jam and jelly should be poured into the jars as soon as possible. Fill the jars to the top as the jam will shrink on cooling. Marmalade and jams which contain whole fruit

(such as some strawberry jams) should be allowed to cool slightly and then stirred to distribute the pieces of peel or the fruit, before being poured into jars. This means that the marmalade or jam is sufficiently set to support the peel or fruit and it won't float to the top. It is a good idea to stand the jars on a large piece of newspaper when filling them. This not only insulates the boiling jam from the cold work surface and so cuts the risk of jars cracking, but also means that any spilt, sticky jam can be cleared away very easily and with the minimum of mess.

Covering and Storing the Jars

As soon as the jars are full, place a well-fitting waxed paper disc over the preserve. If the final covering of the jar with a cellophane, parchment or thin polythene cover is not done immediately, then the jars must be covered with a clean tea towel and put aside until cold and then covered. Fasten the covers with fine string or rubber bands.

Label the jars carefully with the name of the preserve and the date it was made and store them in a cool, dark and airy place.

Recipes

The recipes given may be followed with confidence, but after a while you might want to try your own variations. When mixing fruits, check their pectin content carefully. Never skimp the amount of sugar to be used as sugar is the main preservative. Some people might prefer to use honey in their preserves but unfortunately this prevents a good set and also encourages crystallization.

If the preserve is not to be kept for more than a few weeks however, a jam with a soft set can be made using half sugar and half honey—the flavour certainly makes up for the inconvenience. Honey can be used purely as a flavouring, though, in the same way as spices: use 4 oz. (½ cup) honey to each 3 lb. (6 cups) sugar.

For those of us who are on a diet or diabetic, a few recipes are given for jam set with gelatine. Saccharine, although it sweetens, can not be used in jam making.

Preserves and Conserves are both a type of jam. They contain whole plump fruit. The fruit in preserves is initially boiled in syrup. The fruit for a conserve is mixed with dry sugar before it is boiled.

Trouble-shooting with jams, jellies and marmalades

Mould on the top after storage:
(a) Poor ingredients or recipe used.

(b) The setting test was not done accurately so the set is poor and the yield greater than it should be.

(c) The jar was not filled to the top and the cover was put on while the jam was warm rather than when very hot or when cold.

(d) The jar was stored in a damp place.

Crystals formed on the surface:

(a) Too much acid present (solid mass) or too little acid present ("coffee sugar" crystals).

(b) Fruit not cooked sufficiently before the sugar was added (solid mass) or the fruit was not cooked long enough after the sugar was added ("coffee sugar" crystals).

Preserve shrunken in the jar after storing:

(a) The jar was badly covered and stored in a warm place.

Poor colour and cloudy preserve:

(a) Poor ingredients used.

(b) The preserve was overcooked after adding the sugar.

(c) The scum was not properly removed after cooking.

(d) The jar was stored in a light or warm place.

Tough fruit skins or peel:

(a) The fruit or peel was not cooked until tender, before adding the sugar.

Fruit or peel floating in the jar:

(a) The preserve was not cooled sufficiently before being poured into the jar.

Air bubbles in the preserve:

(a) The preserve was allowed to cool too much before being poured into the jar.

(b) The preserve was poured into the jar too slowly.

Fermented preserve after storing:

(a) Not enough sugar used in the recipe.

(b) Insufficient cooking after the sugar has been added, giving a poor set and a higher yield than there should be.

(c) The opened jar was stored in a warm place.

Cloudy jelly:

(a) The jelly bag was not of a fine enough weave or it was pressed when the juice was dripping through.

Apple Jam

Apple jam can be very uninteresting so is rarely made without some additional flavouring. Apples are, however, rich in pectin, especially when under-ripe and sour, and so can be mixed with fruit that is full-flavoured but contains very little pectin.

Preparing Apples for Preserving

Apple Ginger Jam — Yields about 5 lb.

3 lb. (9 cups peeled and chopped) prepared apples

1 pint (2½ cups) water

2 lemons

2 oz. root ginger (2 medium fresh ginger root)

½ oz. ground ginger

3 lb. (6 cups) white sugar

Peel, core and chop the apples. Reserve the peel and cores.

Place the apples with the water, lemon juice and ground ginger (if used), in the cooking pan. Pare the lemon rind thinly with a sharp knife or potato peeler to remove all the pith. Tie the apple peel and cores, lemon rind and bruised root ginger (if used) in a muslin bag and add to the pan.

Bring to the boil, reduce the heat and simmer until the apple is tender. Remove the muslin bag and squeeze out the juice, then discard.

Add the sugar and stir until dissolved. Boil rapidly until setting point is reached (see page 12). Skim.

Pour the hot jam into hot clean jars. Cover.

Apple and Almond Jam

Make as above, omitting the ginger and adding 2 oz. (⅓ cup) blanched and split almonds with the sugar.

Apple Clove Jam

Make as for Apple Ginger Jam, omitting the ginger and adding 8 whole cloves to the peel and cores in the muslin bag.

Apple and Pear Jam

Make as above using 1½ lb. apples and 1½ lb. pears instead of 3 lb. apples. Omit or include any of the flavourings as liked.

NOTE: If ripe sweet apples are used, do not remove the pith from the lemon rind as this will assist setting.

Apple Jelly

Apple jelly should be made with well-flavoured apples, under-ripe rather than over-ripe, although windfalls can be used. Crab apples also make good jelly. If the flavour of the apples is not particularly good, it is advisable to add some other flavouring as well. Suggestions are given after the recipe.

3 lb. apples
1½–2 pints (3¾–5 cups) water
White sugar

Wash the fruit, remove any bad bits then chop roughly. Place in the cooking pan with just enough water to cover the fruit, bring to the boil and simmer gently for about 1 hour.
Pour the fruit pulp and juice into a jelly bag and drain. Do not press the fruit but allow the juice to strain through, unaided, into a clean bowl.
Test for pectin (see page 11). Measure the juice and allow 1 lb. (2 cups) sugar for each pint (2½ cups) strained juice.
Place the juice and the sugar in the clean cooking pan. Bring to the boil gently, stirring until the sugar is dissolved. Boil rapidly until setting point is reached (see page 12). Skim.
Pour the hot jelly into hot clean jars. Cover.

Apple Ginger Jelly
Place 1–2 oz. bruised root ginger (2 medium fresh ginger root) in a muslin bag and add it to the apples at the beginning of the cooking.

Apple Lemon Jelly
Place the thinly peeled zest from 2 lemons loosely in a muslin bag and add it to the apples at the beginning of the cooking.

Apple Clove Jelly
Place 8 cloves, tied in a muslin bag, in with the apples at the beginning of the cooking time.

Apple Cinnamon Jelly
Place 1 stick of cinnamon, tied in a muslin bag, in with the apples at the beginning of the cooking time.

Apple Geranium Jelly
Place 5 washed rose geranium leaves, tied in a muslin bag, in the strained apple juice before adding the sugar. A few drops of red food colouring can also be added.

Apple Mint Jelly
Cook the apples with the juice of 2 lemons added to the water. Place a bunch of fresh mint, tied loosely in a muslin bag, in with the apples at the beginning of the cooking time. A few drops of green food colouring can be added with the sugar, if liked.

Apple Peppermint Jelly
Cook the apples with the juice of 2 lemons added to the water. Add a few drops of peppermint oil and a few drops of green food colouring, just before setting point is reached.

Pineapple in Apple Jelly
Make the apple jelly as given above and stir in pieces of pineapple just before setting point has been reached. Either canned or ripe fresh pineapple can be used, but do drain canned pineapple thoroughly before adding it to the pan.
Allow the jelly to cool slightly before pouring it into the hot jars so that the pineapple is supported in the jelly and doesn't sink to the bottom. If it is allowed to cool too much, however, you might trap air bubbles in the jelly.

Apple Preserve

Apples are improved by being preserved in a flavoured jelly.

4 lb. (8 cups) white sugar
1½ pints (3¾ cups) water
juice of 2 lemons
4 lb. (12 cups peeled and cubed) prepared apples

Place the sugar and water in the cooking pan, heat gently until boiling, stirring constantly. Remove from the heat and stir in the lemon juice.
Peel and core the apples, cut them into about ½-inch cubes and drop immediately into the prepared syrup.
Bring to the boil and boil for 40 minutes to 1 hour or until the apple is a transparent yellow and the syrup is thick.
Cool slightly before pouring into hot clean jars. Cover.

Apple Ginger Preserve
Tie 4 oz. root ginger (4 medium fresh ginger root) in a muslin bag and add it to the syrup with the lemon juice. Remove the bag, squeezing out any juice, at the end of the cooking time.

Apple Orange Preserve
Omit the lemon juice from the above recipe and use instead the juice and well-washed rind and pith of 2 oranges. Tie the rind and pith loosely in a muslin bag and add it to the syrup with the orange juice. Remove the bag, squeezing out any juice, at the end of the cooking time.

Apricot Jam

3 lb. ripe apricots   Yields about 5 lb.
½–1 pint (1¼–2½ cups) water
juice of 1 lemon
3 lb. (6 cups) white sugar

Wash the apricots, cut in half and remove the stones. Crack about half the stones and remove the kernels. Blanch the kernels by dipping them in boiling water for 1 minute, then removing the skins. Split each kernel in half.

Place the fruit in the cooking pan with ½ pint (1¼ cups) water and the lemon juice. Bring to the boil, reduce the heat and simmer gently until the fruit is tender, adding extra water if necessary. The contents of the pan should be reduced and thickened. Add the blanched kernels.

Add the sugar and stir until dissolved. Boil rapidly until setting point is reached (see page 12), about 10–15 minutes. Skim.

Pour the hot jam into hot clean jars. Cover.

Fresh Apricot and Passion fruit Jam

Yields about 5½ lb.

Make the jam as given above, with the addition of 8 passion fruit. Wash the passion fruit, cut in half and scoop out the seeds and juice. Place the skins in a saucepan and cover with boiling water. Simmer, covered, until soft. Remove the pulp, discarding all the skin and chop the pulp finely. Stir the passion fruit seeds, juice and pulp into the cooked apricots before adding the sugar. Omit the apricot kernels and use only ½ pint (1¼ cups) water.

Dried Apricot Jam

Choose fleshy, full-flavoured fruit for this jam. Dried Peach Jam is made in exactly the same way, substituting peaches for apricots.

1 lb. dried apricots   Yields about 5 lb.
3 pints (7½ cups) water
juice of 1 lemon
3 lb. (6 cups) white sugar
2 oz. (⅓ cup) blanched almonds

Wash the apricots and cut up if desired. Place in a bowl with enough water to cover, cover the bowl with a clean tea towel and leave to soak for at least 24 hours.

Place the soaked fruit in the cooking pan, bring to the boil and simmer for about 30 minutes. Add the lemon juice, sugar and almonds and stir until the sugar is dissolved. Boil rapidly until setting point is reached (see page 12) about 10–15 minutes. Skim.

Pour the hot jam into hot clean jars. Cover.

Apricot Rum Jam

Make apricot jam as given above. Stir in 2 tablespoons (2½T) of rum with the sugar.

Dried Apricot, Apple and Cider Jam

8 oz. dried apricots   Yields about 5 lb.
1 pint (2½ cups) cider
2 lb. (6 cups, peeled and diced) prepared cooking apples
½ pint (1¼ cups) water
1½ tablespoons (1⅞T) lemon juice
3 lb. (6 cups) white sugar

Chop the apricots and place them in a bowl, add the cider. Cover the bowl with a clean tea towel and leave to soak overnight.

Peel, core and dice the apples into ½-inch cubes. Place them in the cooking pan with the soaked apricots, cider, water and lemon juice. Bring to the boil then simmer until the fruit is tender and the contents of the pan reduced.

Add the sugar, stir until dissolved and then boil rapidly until setting point is reached (see page 12). Skim.

Pour the hot jam into hot clean jars and cover.

Apricot and Apple Jam

Make the Dried Apricot, Apple and Cider Jam as given above but use 1 pint (2½ cups) water instead of the cider.

Banana Jam

Yields about 6 lb.

4 lb. (6 medium) peeled bananas
½ pint (1¼ cups) water
4 lemons
3½ lb. (7 cups) white sugar

Peel the bananas, slice them thinly and place in the cooking pan with the water. Cut the lemons in half, squeeze out the juice and add it to the cooking pan. Slice the lemon rind and pith, tie it loosely in a muslin bag, and add it to the pan. Add the sugar, bring to the boil stirring, then simmer 1–2 minutes. Cover the pan with a clean tea towel and put aside overnight.

Next day, bring to the boil again and boil the jam rapidly until setting point is reached (see page 12). Remove the muslin bag and skim.

Pour the hot jam into hot clean jars and cover.

Blackberry Jam

Blackberries are low in acid and pectin and the jam will not set without the addition of other fruit or fruit juice.

3 lb. blackberries   Yields about 5 lb.
4–5 tablespoons (5–6¼T) water
juice of 2 lemons
3 lb. (6 cups) white sugar

Examine the blackberries carefully then place them in the cooking pan with the water and lemon juice. Bring to the boil, reduce the heat and simmer until the fruit is cooked and thickening.
Add the sugar and stir until dissolved. Boil rapidly until setting point is reached (see page 12), about 10–15 minutes. Skim.
Pour the hot jam into hot clean jars. Cover.

Blackberry and Apple Jam

2 lb. blackberries   Yields about 5 lb.
¼ pint (⅝ cup) water
1 lb. (3 medium) cooking apples
3 lb. (6 cups) white sugar

Inspect the blackberries carefully then place in a cooking pan with half the water. Bring to the boil, reduce the heat and simmer gently until the blackberries are cooked and thickening. Meanwhile, peel, core and slice the apples and

place them in a cooking pan with the remaining water. Simmer very gently until soft and pulpy. Add the apple pulp to the blackberries. Add the sugar and stir until dissolved.
Boil rapidly until setting point is reached (see page 12), about 10–15 minutes. Skim.
Pour the hot jam into hot clean jars. Cover.
NOTE: If liked, the cooked blackberries can be pressed through a sieve to remove all the pips. Make sure that only the pips are discarded and that *all* the pulp and juice goes into the jam.

Blackberry and Marrow Jam

1 lb. blackberries   Yields about 6 lb.
3 lb. marrow
½ pint (1¼ cups) water
4 lemons
3½ lb. (7 cups) white sugar

Inspect the blackberries and place in a cooking pan. Peel the marrow and remove the seeds, chop roughly and add to the blackberries with the water, lemon juice and the peel of 1 lemon tied loosely in a muslin bag. Bring to the boil, reduce the heat and simmer gently until the blackberries are tender, the marrow is pulpy and the contents of the pan are thickening. Remove the muslin bag and squeeze out any liquid.
Add the sugar and stir until dissolved. Boil rapidly until setting point is reached (see page 12) about 10–15 minutes. Skim.
Pour the hot jam into hot clean jars. Cover.

Blackberry and Elderberry Jam

2 lb. elderberries   Yields about 5 lb.
8 fl. oz. (1 cup) water
1¾ lb. blackberries
3 lb. (6 cups) white sugar

Remove the elderberries from their stems, wash them and place in a cooking pan with the water. Bring to the boil and simmer gently until soft and pulpy. Press the berries through a sieve to remove the pips. Rinse the cooking pan and return the elderberry pulp and juice to the pan. Inspect the blackberries, place them in the cooking pan and cook them in the elderberry pulp and juice for 10 minutes, or until softened. Add the sugar, stir until dissolved then boil rapidly until setting point is reached (see page 12). Skim.
Pour the hot jam into hot clean jars. Cover.

Blackberry Jelly

4 lb. blackberries
juice of 2 lemons
¾ pint (scant 2 cups) water
white sugar

Wash the blackberries and put them in the cooking pan with the lemon juice and water. Bring to the boil then reduce the heat and simmer very gently until the fruit is tender.

Mash the blackberries then pour the juice and pulp into a jelly bag and allow to drain. Do not press the fruit but allow the juice to strain through unaided into a clean bowl.

Test for pectin (see page 11). Measure the juice and allow 1 lb. (2 cups) sugar for each pint (2½ cups) juice.

Place the sugar and juice in the clean cooking pan. Bring slowly to the boil, stirring until the sugar is dissolved. Boil rapidly until setting point is reached (see page 12). Skim.

Pour the hot jelly into hot clean jars. Cover.

Blackberry and Apple Jelly
2 lb. blackberries
1 lb. (3 medium) cooking apples (washed and chopped)
1 pint (2½ cups) water
white sugar

Make the jelly as given in the previous recipe, cooking the blackberries with half the water in one pan and the washed and chopped apples with the remaining water in a separate pan. The apples should be pulpy and very tender. The two fruits can be mixed for draining the juice.

Spiced Blackberry Jelly
Make the jelly as described. Put 4 cloves and 1 small stick of cinnamon in a muslin bag and place in the blackberries at the beginning of the cooking time. Add 2 tablespoons (2½ T) wine vinegar with each pound (2 cups) of sugar.

NOTE: Try serving this jelly with cold meat as well as on the tea table.

Black Currant Jam

The most common fault of this jam is tough fruit. Make sure that the initial cooking is thorough, tasting the currants occasionally to see that they are well cooked. Avoid using a copper cooking pan.

2 lb. black currants   Yields about 5 lb.
1½ pints (3¾ cups) water
3 lb. (6 cups) white sugar

Cooking Fruit for Making Jam

Remove the currants from the stems and wash them. Place them in the cooking pan with the water. Bring to the boil, reduce the heat and simmer gently until the fruit is tender and the contents of the pan are well reduced and thickening. Stir occasionally.

Add the sugar, stir until dissolved then boil rapidly until setting point is reached (see page 12). Skim.

Pour the hot jam into hot clean jars. Cover.

Black Currant and Apple Jam

Make as for cherry jam. Tie 1 stick of cinnamon 12 oz. peeled, cored and thinly sliced apple to the recipe. Cook the black currants in 1 pint (2½ cups) of the water and the apple in a separate pan with the remaining ½ pint (1¼ cups) water. Mix the fruit together when both are very tender, immediately before adding the sugar.

Cherry Jam

Cherry jam has the reputation of being difficult to make. Cherries are low in pectin compared with other stone fruit but you can achieve a very good result by adding acid and by using a higher proportion than usual of fruit to sugar. The variety "May Duke" makes the best jam, with "Morello" and other of the more acid varieties a close second. Black cherries tend to make a very sweet jam which is nearer the traditional Swiss cherry jam.

The cherry stones can be removed before cooking or the cherries can be cut in half so that the stones come out during cooking. They can then be skimmed off the top with a slotted spoon.

5 lb. cherries (about 5½ lb. before the stones are removed) Yields about 6 lb.
juice of 3 lemons (if Morello cherries are used, use only 1½ lemons)
water if necessary
3½ lb. (7 cups) white sugar

Wash the cherries, remove the stones if liked (see above) and tie the stones in a muslin bag. Place the cherries, stones and lemon juice in the cooking pan with a little water is necessary. Heat very gently, stirring occasionally until just simmering. Simmer for 30 minutes or until the cherries are tender. Remove the stones if in a muslin bag.

Add the sugar, stir until it is dissolved and the jam is boiling. Skim off the stones as they rise to the surface. Boil rapidly until setting point is reached (see page 12). Skim again.

Pour the hot jam into hot clean jars. Cover.

Cherry and Orange Jam Yields about 8 lb. Make as for cherry jam, using black cherries and with the addition of oranges. Wash 4 seedless, sweet oranges, cut them into very thin slices. Place the rounds in a cooking pan with enough water to cover. Simmer gently until the orange rind is very tender. Add the orange to the cooked cherries with the sugar.

Spiced Cherry Jam Yields about 6 lb. Make as for cherry jam. Tie 1 stick of cinnamon and 8 cloves in a muslin bag and add to the cherries at the beginning of cooking time. Remove the bag when the sugar is added. Some of the cherry stones can be cracked and the kernels blanched by plunging them into boiling water. Add the kernels to the cooked cherries with the sugar.

Cherry Conserve

4 lb. stoned cherries (about 4½ lb. unstoned) Yields about 6 lb.
3½ lb. (7 cups) white sugar
2 lemons

Wash the cherries, remove the stones and place in a bowl in layers with the sugar. Cover with a clean tea towel and put aside for 24 hours.

Peel the lemons and squeeze out the juice. Tie the lemon peel and pith loosely in a muslin bag. Place the cherry and sugar mixture in the cooking pan with the lemon juice and the bag of peel. Bring to the boil, stirring frequently. Boil until setting point is reached (see page 12). Remove and squeeze the muslin bag. Skim.

Cool slightly before spooning into hot clean jars. Cover.

Cherry Preserve

Cherries are low in pectin, so for a firm preserve either use additional commercial pectin or add red currant juice to the syrup. Without either of these, the set will be very light but still acceptable. Use Morello cherries for the best results but black cherries with added lemon juice are also good.

4 lb. stoned cherries (about 4½ lb. unstoned) Yields about 7 lb.
4 lb. (8 cups) white sugar
1½ pints (3¾ cups) water
1½ pints (3¾ cups) red currant juice

Wash the cherries and remove the stones. Place the sugar and water in a cooking pan and bring to the boil, stirring constantly. Add the cherries and bring to the boil again, stirring gently. Boil for 5 minutes. Skim, remove from the heat and put aside for 24 hours.

Add the red currant juice and boil the preserve for 5 minutes.

Spoon the cherries into hot clean jars with a slotted spoon. Bring the remaining syrup to the boil and boil until setting point is reached (see page 12). Skim. Fill jars with syrup and cover.

Black Cherry Preserve

Make as for Cherry Preserve (see opposite), omitting the red currant juice and using an extra 1½ pints (3¾ cups) water. Add the juice of 2 lemons to the water and the peel and pith of a lemon, tied loosely in a muslin bag. Remove the bag when the cherries are spooned into the jars.

Chinese Gooseberry Jam

Chinese gooseberries are low in pectin and are usually combined with citrus fruits when making jam.

Chinese Gooseberry and Grapefruit Jam

Yields about 5 lb.

3 lb. Chinese gooseberries (prepared)
1 grapefruit
1 lemon
3 lb. (6 cups) white sugar

Peel the Chinese gooseberries and chop roughly. Squeeze the juice from the grapefruit and lemon. If the pith is very thick, remove and discard some of it, otherwise tie the peel, skin, pips (seeds) and pith loosely in a muslin bag.

Place the Chinese gooseberries in the cooking pan with the fruit juice and the muslin bag. Bring to the boil very slowly, stirring occasionally, then simmer very gently until the fruit is softened. Add the sugar and stir until dissolved. Boil briskly until setting point is reached (see page 12), about 15–20 minutes. Remove the muslin bag. Skim.

Pour the hot jam into hot clean jars. Cover.

Cranberry Jam

2 lb. cranberries   Yields about 3 lb.
¼ pint (⅝ cup) water
1¾ lb. (3½ cups) white sugar

Wash the cranberries, drain well then place them in the cooking pan with the water. Bring to the boil. Reduce the heat and simmer until the cranberries are tender.

Add the sugar, bring to the boil again, stirring until the sugar is dissolved. Boil rapidly until setting point is reached (see page 12). Skim. Pour the jam into hot clean jars. Cover.

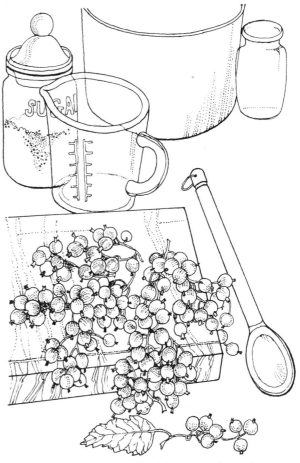

Currant Jelly (Black, Red or White Currants)

2 lb. black currants or 3 lb. red or white currants
1 pint (2½ cups) water
white sugar

Wash the currants, but there is no need to remove them from the stems. Place them in the cooking pan with the water, bring to the boil and simmer gently until the fruit is tender. Mash very well. Pour the juice and pulp into a jelly bag and allow to drain. Do not press the fruit but allow the juice to strain through unaided into a clean bowl.

Test for pectin (see page 11). Measure the juice and allow 1 lb. (2 cups) sugar for each pint (2½ cups) strained juice.

Place the sugar and juice in the clean cooking pan. Heat gently, stirring until the sugar is dissolved. Boil rapidly until setting point is reached (see page 12). Skim.

Pour the hot jelly into hot clean jars. Cover.

Currant and Raspberry Jelly

Make as for Currant Jelly, using 2 or 3 lb. of currants (according to the colour) and an equal weight of raspberries. Do not increase the water.

Damson Jam

2½ lb. damsons   Yields about 5 lb.
¾–1 pint (2–2½ cups) water
3 lb. (6 cups) white sugar

Wash the damsons and place in the cooking pan with the water. Bring to the boil then reduce the heat and simmer slowly until the damsons are well cooked and broken down.
Add the sugar and stir until dissolved. Bring to the boil, remove the stones with a slotted spoon as they rise to the surface. Boil rapidly until setting point is reached (see page 12). Skim.
Pour the hot jam into hot clean jars. Cover.

Damson Jelly

3 lb. damsons
1½ pints (3¾ cups) water
white sugar

Wash the damsons and place them in the cooking pan with the water. Bring to the boil and simmer until the fruit is very tender. Mash the damsons well then pour the pulp and fruit into a jelly bag and allow to drain. Do not press the fruit but allow the juice to strain through unaided.
Test for pectin (see page 11). Measure the strained juice and allow 1 lb. (2 cups) sugar to each pint (2½ cups) strained juice. Place the sugar and juice in the clean cooking pan. Heat gently, stirring until the sugar is dissolved. Boil rapidly until setting point is reached (see page 12). Skim.
Pour the hot jelly into hot clean jars. Cover.

Elderberry Jelly

Elderberries are low both in acid and pectin. If you want to make pure elderberry jelly, add about 1½ tablespoons (2T) lemon juice to each pound of berries at the beginning of cooking time; then add commercial pectin as directed on the packet or bottle. The extra acid and pectin do, however, tend to mask the flavour of the elderberries. The following recipe will produce a jelly with an excellent flavour.

Elderberry and Apple Jelly
2 lb. elderberries
2 lb. apples
water
white sugar

Wash the fruit, place the elderberries in one pan and the apples, sliced, in another. Add water to cover the elderberries and apples, then bring to the boil and simmer, separately, until very tender.

Pour the pulp and liquid into a jelly bag and allow to drain. Do not press the fruit but allow the juice to strain through unaided.
Test for pectin (see page 11). Measure the juice and allow 12 oz. (1½ cups) sugar for each pint (2½ cups) strained juice. Place the juice and the sugar in a clean cooking pan and bring slowly to the boil, stirring until the sugar is dissolved. Boil rapidly until setting point is reached (see page 12). Skim.
Pour the hot jelly into hot clean jars. Cover.

Fig Jam

Both fresh and dried figs can be made into a delicious and unusual jam. Under-ripe fresh figs should be used in preference to ripe ones.

       Making Apricot Jam

Fresh Fig Jam
Yields about 5 lb.
4 lb. fresh figs
½ pint (1¼ cups) water
juice of 4 lemons
rind and pith of 2 lemons
3 lb. (6 cups) white sugar

Wash the figs, remove the stalks and slice. Place in a cooking pan with the water and lemon juice, and the lemon rind and pith, tied loosely in a muslin bag. Bring to the boil, reduce the heat and simmer until the figs are tender.

Remove the muslin bag. Add the sugar and stir until dissolved. Boil rapidly until setting point is reached (see page 12), about 20 minutes. Skim. Pour the hot jam into hot clean jars. Cover.

Dried Fig Jam
Yields about 5 lb.
2 lb. dried figs
1½ pints (3¾ cups) water
6 tablespoons (7½ T) lemon juice
3 lb. (6 cups) white sugar

Place the figs in a bowl with water to cover; soak for at least 12 hours. Drain the figs and rinse them in fresh water. Cut out the stem and chop roughly. Place in the cooking pan with the water and lemon juice. Bring to the boil and simmer gently until the figs are tender.

Add the sugar and stir until dissolved. Boil rapidly until the contents of the pan have thickened.

Pour the hot jam into hot clean jars. Cover.

Fig and Apple Jam

Make as for Fresh Fig Jam (see page 25), but use 3 lb. figs and 1 lb. peeled, cored and sliced apples instead of all figs. Cook the prepared apples in half water in a separate pan until soft and pulpy. Mix the two cooked fruits together before adding the sugar.

Guava Jelly

2½ lb. guavas
8 oz. apples
2 lemons
white sugar

Wash the fruit. Quarter the guavas, slice the apples and lemons. Place the fruit in a cooking pan with just enough water to cover. Bring to the boil and simmer until the fruit is very tender, about 45 minutes.

Mash the fruit then pour the pulp and juice into a jelly bag. Allow the juice to strain through into a clean bowl, unaided. Do not press the pulp.

Test for pectin (see page 11). Measure the juice and allow 1 lb. (2 cups) sugar to each ¾ pint (2 cups) strained juice.

Place the juice and sugar in the clean cooking pan, bring to the boil, stirring until the sugar is dissolved. Boil rapidly until setting point is reached (see page 12). Skim.

Pour the hot jelly into hot clean jars. Cover.

Gooseberry Jam

The colour of the finished jam will depend mainly on the variety and ripeness of the gooseberries used. The colour of a reddish jam will be deepened with long cooking. Green gooseberry jam will have a better colour if a copper cooking pan is used.

2¼ lb. gooseberries   Yields about 5 lb.
¾ pint (scant 2 cups) water
3 lb. (6 cups) white sugar

Wash the gooseberries, top and tail them and place in the cooking pan with the water. Bring to the boil, reduce the heat and simmer gently until the fruit is soft and broken down, about 45 minutes.

Add the sugar, stir until dissolved. Boil briskly until setting point is reached (see page 12). Skim.
Pour the hot jam into hot clean jars. Cover.

Gooseberry and Elderflower Jam

Pick the flowers from 12 heads of elderflower and tie them loosely in a muslin bag. Add to the gooseberries at the beginning of the cooking time and remove just before adding sugar.

Gooseberry and Red Currant Jam

Yields about 5 lb.
Make as for Gooseberry Jam, using 1 lb. red currants (removed from the stalks) and 1¼ lb. gooseberries, instead of all gooseberries.

Gooseberry Jelly

As for jam, use a copper pan for cooking the gooseberries and a better green colour will result. Extra food colouring may be added to the juice if necessary, just before setting point.

4 lb. green gooseberries
2 pints (5 cups) water
white sugar

Wash the gooseberries and place them in the cooking pan with the water. Bring to the boil and simmer gently until the gooseberries are very tender.

Mash the fruit thoroughly then pour the pulp and juice into a jelly bag. Allow the juice to drain through into a clean bowl without pressing the fruit.

Test for pectin (see page 11). Measure the juice and allow 1 lb. (2 cups) sugar for each pint (2½ cups) sugar.

Place the strained juice and sugar in the clean cooking pan and heat slowly until boiling. Stir until the sugar is dissolved. Boil rapidly until setting point is reached (see page 12). Skim.
Pour the hot jelly into hot clean jars. Cover.

Gooseberry and Currant Jelly

Make as for Gooseberry Jelly, using 2 lb. green gooseberries and 2 lb. currants.

Grape Jam

Additional acid in the form of lemon juice is nearly always added to the grapes when making jam. If the grapes are under-ripe and sour however, the lemon juice can be omitted.

3 lb. (Concord) grapes   Yields about 4½ lb.
juice of 2 small lemons
¼ pint (⅝ cup) water
2½ lb. (5 cups) white sugar

Wash the grapes, remove the skins if very tough. Place them in the cooking pan and crush lightly with a wooden spoon. Add the lemon juice and water, bring gently to the boil and simmer, stirring frequently, until the grapes are softened, about 10 minutes. Skim the seeds off the surface. Add the sugar, stir until dissolved. Boil rapidly until setting point is reached (see page 12). Skim.
Pour the hot jam into hot clean jars. Cover.

Grape and Orange Jam

Make the jam as above using slightly under-ripe grapes and substituting orange juice for the lemon juice. The orange rind, finely grated, can be added to the grapes before cooking.

Grape Jelly

4 lb. green grapes
½ pint (1¼ cups) water
white sugar

Wash the grapes and place in the cooking pan with the water. Bring to the boil and simmer gently until the fruit is very tender.
Mash the fruit well then pour the pulp and juice into a jelly bag. Allow the fruit to drain. Do not press it but let the juice strain through unaided into a clean bowl.
Test for pectin (see page 11). Measure the strained juice and allow 1 lb. (2 cups) sugar for each pint (2½ cups) juice.
Place the juice and sugar into the clean cooking pan, bring slowly to the boil, stirring until the sugar is dissolved. Boil rapidly until setting point is reached (see page 12). Skim.
Pour the hot jelly into hot clean jars. Cover.

Spiced Grape Jelly

Make as for Grape Jelly. Add 8 cloves *or* 1 stick cinnamon, tied in a muslin bag, to the grapes at the beginning of the cooking.

Greengage Jam

3 lb. greengages   Yields about 5 lb.
¼–¾ pint (⅝ cup–2 cups) water
3 lb. (6 cups) white sugar

Wash the fruit, cut in halves and remove the stones. Place in the cooking pan with ¼ pint (⅝ cup) water. Crack some of the stones, remove the kernels and blanch them in boiling water for 1 minute; then remove the skins and split in half. Add the kernels to the pan, bring to the boil and simmer until the greengages are tender and the contents of the pan well-reduced. Add extra water if necessary.
Add the sugar, stir until dissolved. Boil rapidly until setting point is reached (see page 12). Skim.
Pour the hot jam into hot clean jars. Cover.

Japonica Jam

4 lb. japonicas   Yields about 6 lb.
6 pints (15 cups) water
white sugar
juice of 4 lemons

Chop the japonicas roughly and place them in the cooking pan with the water. Bring to the boil and simmer until very soft and pulpy. Press the pulp through a sieve to remove all the cores and husks.
Weigh the sieved pulp and allow 12 oz. (1½ cups) sugar to each pound of pulp. Rinse the cooking pan and place the weighed pulp, sugar and lemon juice in the clean pan. Bring to the boil, stirring until the sugar is dissolved. Boil rapidly until setting point is reached (see page 12). Skim.
Pour the hot jam into hot clean jars. Cover.

Spiced Japonica Jam

Make as for Japonica Jam. Add either 1 teaspoon ground cloves *or* 1 teaspoon ground cinnamon to the cooking pan with the lemon juice.

Loganberry Jam

3 lb. loganberries   Yields about 5 lb.
3 lb. (6 cups) white sugar

Place the fruit in a cooking pan and heat gently, stirring frequently. Simmer gently until the fruit is softened and the juice is running out.
Add the sugar, stirring until dissolved. Bring to the boil and boil briskly until setting point is reached (see page 12). Skim.
Pour the hot jam into hot clean jars. Cover.
NOTE: The varieties on this jam are the same as for raspberry jam (see page 38).

Loganberry Jelly

If the loganberries are very ripe, add 1 tablespoon (1¼ T) lemon juice at the beginning of the cooking time.

4 lb. loganberries
1 pint (2½ cups) water
white sugar

Wash the loganberries and place in the cooking pan with the water. Bring to the boil and simmer until tender.
Mash the fruit well then pour the pulp and juice into a jelly bag. Allow the juice to strain through unaided into a clean bowl.
Test for pectin (see page 11). Measure the juice and allow 1 lb. (2 cups) sugar for each pint (2½ cups) strained juice.
Place the juice and sugar in a clean cooking pan and bring slowly to the boil, stirring until the sugar is dissolved. Boil rapidly until setting point is reached (see page 12). Skim.
Pour the hot jelly into hot clean jars. Cover.

Overleaf: Pineapple in Apple Jelly

Apple +
Pineapple

Mint Jelly

This recipe varies from that for Apple Mint Jelly (see page 17). It produces a piquant jelly which is more acceptable with roast lamb.

3 lb. green apples
1 pint (2½ cups) water
small bunch of fresh mint
1¼ pints (good 3 cups) white malt vinegar
white sugar
3 tablespoons (3¾T) finely chopped mint
green food colouring

Wash the apples, cut them in quarters and place in a cooking pan with the water. Wash the bunch of mint and add it to the cooking pan. Bring to the boil then simmer gently until the apples are soft and pulpy. Stir in the vinegar and boil for 5 minutes.

Pour the apple pulp and the liquid into a jelly bag and allow the juice to strain through into a clean bowl. Do not press or squeeze the fruit.

Test for pectin (see page 11). Measure the juice and allow 1 lb. (2 cups) sugar for each pint (2½ cups) strained juice.

Place the juice and sugar in a clean cooking pan. Bring gently to the boil, stirring until the sugar is dissolved. Add the chopped mint and a few drops of green food colouring, as necessary. Boil rapidly until setting point is reached (see page 12). Skim.

Pour the hot jelly into hot clean jars. Cover.

Marrow (marrow squash) Jam

Marrows (marrow squash) need extra flavouring before they can be made into interesting jam. They do have a distinct flavour of their own, however, and this is usually strongest in the large, late-season marrows. Take care not to overcook the jam as it tends to become sugary with storage.

Marrow and Ginger Jam

Yields about 5 lb.
4 lb. (about 5 lb.) prepared marrow
   (marrow squash)
3 lb. (6 cups) white sugar
3 tablespoons (3¾T) lemon juice
2 oz. root ginger (2 medium fresh ginger
   root) or 2 teaspoons ground ginger

Peel the marrow, remove the seeds and cut into dice. Place in a steamer and cook over simmering water until just tender.

Place the cooked marrow in a bowl and sprinkle the sugar over the top. Cover the bowl with a clean tea towel and leave for 12 hours.

Next day place the marrow, sugar, lemon juice and ginger in the cooking pan. If using root ginger, crush it with a mallet or rolling pin and place it in a muslin bag before adding to the cooking pan. Bring slowly to the boil, reduce the heat and cook very gently, stirring occasionally, for about 1 hour. The marrow should be transparent and the contents of the pan thickened and reduced. Test for setting, but the result will not be very positive. Weighing the pan of jam will give a more definite indication as to whether or not the jam is ready (see page 12). Remove the bag of root ginger, if used. Skim.

Pour the hot jam into hot clean jars. Cover.

Marrow and Lemon Jam
Make as for Marrow (marrow squash) and Ginger Jam. A better set will be achieved if the juice of 3 lemons is used and the peel and pith are tied loosely in the muslin bag with the root ginger.

Marrow Conserve

Make in the same way as Cherry Conserve (see page 22), substituting marrow (marrow squash) for the cherries. Cut the marrow (marrow squash) into cubes. Bruise 2 oz. root ginger (2 medium fresh ginger root) and add it to the lemon peel in the muslin bag.

Melon Conserve

Make in the same way as Cherry Conserve (see page 22), substituting melon for the cherries. Peel the melon and cut it into cubes. Bruise 2 oz. root ginger and add it to the lemon peel in the muslin bag.

Pear Conserve

Make in the same way as Cherry Conserve (see page 22), substituting pear for the cherries. Peel and core the pears before weighing, then cut them into cubes or slice them. Hard pears may need gentle cooking to soften them before using. Bruise 2 oz. root ginger (2 medium fresh ginger root) and add it to the lemon peel in the muslin bag.

Mulberry Jam

2 lb. mulberries   Yields about 3½ lb.
¼ pint (⅝ cup) water
juice of 2 lemons
2 lb. (4 cups) white sugar

Place the mulberries in a cooking pan with the water and lemon juice. Heat slowly until simmering, then cook gently until the fruit is

softened.
Add the sugar and stir until dissolved. Bring to the boil and boil rapidly until setting point is reached (see page 12). Skim.
Pour the hot jam into hot clean jars. Cover.

Seedless Mulberry Jam

Make as for Mulberry Jam. Before adding the sugar, sieve the cooked fruit to remove all the seeds. Make sure that all the pulp and juice is returned to the clean pan; only the seeds must be discarded.

Mulberry and Apple Jam

1¼ lb. mulberries   Yields about 3 lb.
12 oz. (2 cups) peeled and sliced apples
8 fl. oz. (1 cup) water
juice of 1 lemon
1¾ lb. (3½ cups) white sugar

Place the mulberries in the cooking pan with the peeled, cored and sliced apples, water and lemon juice. Heat slowly until simmering then cook gently until the fruit is softened.
Add the sugar, stir until dissolved. Boil rapidly until setting point is reached, (see page 12). Skim.
Pour the hot jam into hot clean jars. Cover.

Passion Fruit Jam

24 passion fruit   Yields about 4 lb.
8 fl. oz. (1 cup) water
2 tablespoons (2½T) lemon juice
2½ lb. (5 cups) white sugar

Wash the passion fruit, cut in half and scoop out the pulp and seeds. Reserve half the skins and place in a bowl with enough water to cover. Cover the bowl with a clean tea towel and leave for 12 hours.

Next day, place the soaked shells and the water in a saucepan, bring to the boil and simmer for about 30 minutes or until the skins are tender. Scoop out the pulp and discard any remaining skin.

Chop the pulp finely and place it in the cooking pan with the fruit pulp and seeds, water and lemon juice.

Add the sugar, stir until dissolved. Bring to the boil and boil rapidly until setting point is reached (see page 12). Allow the jam to cool slightly before pouring into hot clean jars. Cover when cold.

Peach Jam

4 lb. peaches   Yields about 6 lb.
$\frac{3}{4}$ pint (2 cups) water
juice of 2 lemons
pith of 1 lemon
$3\frac{3}{4}$ lb. ($7\frac{1}{2}$ cups) white sugar

Wash the peaches, cut up, remove the stones and place in the cooking pan. Crack a few of the stones, remove the kernels and blanch them by dipping in a pan of boiling water for a few minutes, rinsing them in cold water and slipping off the skins. Add the blanched kernels to the cooking pan with the lemon juice and the lemon pith, tied loosely in a muslin bag.

Bring to the boil, reduce the heat and simmer until the peaches and skins are very tender.

Add the sugar, stir until dissolved. Boil rapidly until setting point is reached (see page 12). Skim. Pour the hot jam into hot clean jars. Cover.

Peach and Pear Jam

Make as for Peach Jam, but use half peaches and half pears. The addition of the juice and pith of an extra lemon will help with the setting.

Dried Peach Jam

Make as for Dried Apricot Jam (see recipe page 18), using dried peaches instead of apricots.

Pear Jam

Pears are low in pectin and acid so a lot of both needs to be added before the jam will set successfully. Increase the amount of water and the cooking time if under-ripe pears are used.

Yields about $4\frac{1}{4}$ lb.

3 lb. prepared pears (about 9 pears)
$\frac{1}{4}$–$\frac{3}{4}$ pint ($\frac{5}{8}$–2 cups) water
juice of 3 lemons
pith of 2 small lemons
$2\frac{1}{2}$ lb. (5 cups) white sugar

Peel and core the pears, chop them and place in the cooking pan with the water and lemon juice and the lemon pith, tied loosely in a muslin bag. Heat slowly then simmer until the fruit is tender. Remove the bag of pith.

Add the sugar and stir until dissolved. Bring to the boil and boil rapidly until setting point is reached (see page 12). Skim.

Pour the hot jam into hot clean jars. Cover.

Pear and Ginger Jam
Pear and Almond Jam
Pear Clove Jam

Make these jams using the basic Pear Jam recipe, and adding the flavourings as for Apple Jam. (See recipe page 16).

Pear and Apricot Jam

Yields about 7 lb.

1 lb. prepared pears (about 3 pears)
1 lb. apricots
about $\frac{1}{2}$ pint ($1\frac{1}{4}$ cups) water
4 lemons
4 lb. (8 cups) white sugar

Peel, core and slice the pears. Wash the apricots, cut them in half, remove the stones and place them with the prepared pears and the water in the cooking pan. Cut the lemons in half, squeeze out the juice and add it to the pan. Slice the skins and tie them loosely in a muslin bag. Place the bag in the pan. Bring the contents of the pan to the boil then reduce the heat and simmer gently until the fruit is tender and the mixture is beginning to thicken. Remove the muslin bag. Add the sugar, stir until dissolved and then boil rapidly until setting point is reached (see page 12). Skim.

Pour the hot jam into hot clean jars and cover.

Pear and Ginger Preserve

Yields about 4 lb.

4 lb. prepared pears (about 12 pears)
1 tablespoon ($1\frac{1}{4}$T) lemon juice
6 cloves
$2\frac{1}{4}$ lb. ($4\frac{1}{2}$ cups) white sugar
$1\frac{1}{4}$ pints ($3\frac{1}{2}$ cups) water
4 oz. preserved ginger (in syrup)

Peel, core and slice the pears. Place them in a dish with the lemon juice and cloves. Put aside for about 30 minutes.

Meanwhile, place the sugar in the cooking pan with the water. Bring to the boil, stirring until the sugar is dissolved. Boil for 8 minutes.

Add the pears to the syrup. Bring to the boil again and simmer gently until the pears are

tender and the liquid syrupy.

Chop the ginger into pieces, slice the orange rind into matchstick-thin strips. Add the ginger and orange rind to the pears and return to the boil.

Pour the hot preserve into hot clean jars and cover.

Pineapple Jam

Pineapples contain a high proportion of acid but very little pectin so it is more important to include the rind and pith of the lemons, which are rich in pectin, than the lemon juice.

4 lb. pineapple   Yields about 7 lb.
1 pint (2½ cups) water
juice of 2 lemons
rind and pith of 4 lemons
4 lb. (8 cups) white sugar

Peel and dice the pineapple. Place in the cooking pan with the water, lemon juice and lemon rind and pith, tied loosely in a muslin bag. Bring to the boil and simmer until the pineapple is very tender. Cool. Pour into a bowl, stir in the sugar, cover with a clean towel or tea towel and leave for 12 hours. Remove the muslin bag of rinds and pith.

Next day return all to the cooking pan and heat, stirring until the sugar is well dissolved. Boil rapidly until setting point is reached (see page 12). Skim.

Pour the hot jam into hot clean jars. Cover.

Pineapple Conserve

4 lb. pineapple   Yields about 7 lb.
4 lb. (8 cups) white sugar
2 lemons

Remove the peel and core from the pineapple and cut it into chunks. Place the pineapple and sugar in a bowl in alternate layers. Cover the bowl with a clean towel or tea towel and put aside for 24 hours.

Peel the lemon and place the peel, including the pith, in a muslin bag. Pour the pineapple and sugar mixture into a cooking pan and add the bag of peel. Bring to the boil, stirring frequently and boil until setting point is reached (see page 12). Skim.

Cool slightly before spooning into hot clean jars. Cover.

Plum Jam

The amount of water needed for plum jam will vary according to how ripe and juicy the plums are.

3 lb. plums   Yields about 5 lb.
¼–¾ pint (⅝–2 cups) water
3 lb. (6 cups) white sugar

Wash the plums, cut in half and remove the stones. Crack some of the stones and remove the kernels. Place the plums, kernels and water in the cooking pan, bring to the boil and simmer until the plum skins are softened.

Add the sugar, stir until dissolved. Bring to the boil and boil rapidly until setting point is reached (see page 12). Skim.

Pour the hot jam into hot clean jars. Cover.

NOTE: The stones can be left in the fruit halves until the sugar has been added. The stones will then rise to the surface and as many as possible can be skimmed off with a slotted spoon.

Plum and Apple Jam

Make as for Plum Jam, using half plums and half apples.

Cinnamon Plum Jam

Make as for Plum Jam, adding 1 teaspoon ground cinnamon with the sugar.

Quince Jam

2 lb. quinces (prepared)   Yields about 5 lb.
2 pints (5 cups) water
juice of 1 lemon
3 lb. (6 cups) white sugar

Peel, core and grate the quinces into the cooking pan. Add the water, bring to the boil and simmer gently until the fruit is tender. This will take about 20 minutes. The contents of the pan should be reduced and thickening.

Add the lemon juice and sugar, stir until the sugar is dissolved. Boil rapidly until setting point is reached (see page 12). Skim.

Pour the hot jam into hot clean jars. Cover.

Quince Jelly

2 lb. quinces
3 pints (7½ cups) water
8 tablespoons (10T) lemon juice
white sugar

Wash the quinces, chop roughly and place them in the cooking pan with the water and lemon juice. Bring to the boil and simmer covered until the fruit is very tender (about 1–1½ hours). Pour the pulp and juice into a jelly bag and allow to drain. Do not press or squeeze the bag but allow the juice to strain through, unaided, into a clean bowl.

Test for pectin (see page 11). Measure the juice and allow 1 lb. (2 cups) sugar for each pint (2½ cups) strained juice.

Place the juice and sugar in the clean cooking pan. Bring to the boil, stirring until the sugar is dissolved; boil rapidly until setting point is reached (see page 12). Skim.

Pour the hot jelly into hot clean jars. Cover.

Raspberry Conserve

Use raspberries which are firm, ripe and bright red in colour.

4 lb. raspberries
4 lb. (8 cups) white sugar
2 lemons

Inspect the raspberries carefully and place them and the sugar in a bowl in alternate layers. Cover the bowl with a clean towel or tea towel and put aside for 24 hours.

Peel the lemons and squeeze out the juice. Tie the peel and pith in a muslin bag. Place the raspberry and sugar mixture in the cooking pan with the lemon juice and the bag of peel and pith. Bring to the boil, stirring frequently, and boil

Using Raspberry Jelly (left)
Rhubarb Jam (below)

until setting point is reached (see page 12). Skim.

Cool slightly before pouring into hot clean jars. Cover.

Raspberry Jam

3 lb. raspberries   Yields about 5 lb.
3 lb. (6 cups) white sugar

Inspect the fruit carefully. Place it in the cooking pan and heat very gently until some of the juice has come out. Simmer until the raspberries are softened and tender.

Add the sugar, stir until dissolved. Bring to the boil and boil rapidly until setting point is reached (see page 12). Skim.

Pour the hot jam into hot clean jars. Cover.

Seedless Raspberry Jam
Make as for Raspberry Jam. Press the cooked raspberries through a sieve and discard the seeds. Make sure that *all* the pulp and juice is returned to the rinsed cooking pan before adding the sugar.

Raspberry and Red currant Jam
Make as for Raspberry Jam, but using half raspberries and half red currants. Up to ½ pint (1¼ cups) water may be needed when cooking the fruit.

Special Raspberry Jam

2 lb. raspberries   Yields about 5 lb.
½–¾ pint (1¼–2 cups) pure raspberry and red currant juice
2 tablespoons (2½T) lemon juice
3 lb. (6 cups) white sugar

Inspect the raspberries and place them in the cooking pan with the fruit juice and lemon juice. Bring to the boil and simmer gently until the raspberries are tender, about 15–20 minutes. Add the sugar, stir until dissolved. Boil rapidly until setting point is reached (see page 12). Skim.

Pour the hot jam into hot clean jars. Cover.

NOTE: The fruit juice should be made by crushing and straining the raw fruit. No water must be added.

Raspberry Jelly

4 lb. raspberries
1 tablespoon (1¼T) water
white sugar

Place the raspberries in the cooking pan with the water. Simmer very gently until the raspberries are very soft. Mash well.

Pour the pulp and juice into a jelly bag and allow to drain without pressing or squeezing.

Test for pectin (see page 11). Measure the juice and allow 1 lb. (2 cups) sugar for each pint (2½ cups) juice.

Place the strained juice and the sugar in a cooking pan and heat gently until boiling, stirring until the sugar is dissolved. Boil rapidly until setting point is reached. Skim.

Pour the hot jelly into hot clean jars. Cover.

Raspberry and Red currant Jelly
Make as for Raspberry Jelly using 2 lb. raspberries and 2 lb. red currants. Cook the fruit together in ¾ pint (scant 2 cups) water.

The yield and set for this jelly are better than for raspberry jelly on its own.

Rhubarb Jam

The rhubarb that appears late in the season has more flavour than that of early spring.

3 lb. rhubarb stalks   Yields about 5 lb.
3 lemons
1 tablespoon (1¼T) water
3 lb. (6 cups) white sugar

Trim the rhubarb and cut into chunks. Place it in the cooking pan with the lemon juice and water and the lemon rind and pith, tied loosely in a muslin bag. Bring to the boil slowly and simmer until tender.

Add the sugar and stir until dissolved. Remove the muslin bag. Boil rapidly until setting point is reached (see page 12). Skim.

Pour the hot jam into hot clean jars. Cover.

Rhubarb and Ginger Jam
Make as for Rhubarb Jam. Add 1 oz. root ginger (1 medium fresh ginger root), crushed, to the peel and pith in the muslin bag *or* sprinkle 1 teaspoon ground ginger onto the cooked rhubarb, before adding the sugar.

Rhubarb and Orange Jam
Make as for Rhubarb Jam (see above). Omit the lemons and use instead the juice and rinds of 5 oranges. The juice and the rinds and pith tied loosely in a muslin bag, should be added to the rhubarb in the cooking pan.

Rhubarb and Raspberry Jam

1½ lb. rhubarb stalks   Yields about 5 lb.
¼ pint (⅝ cup) water
1 lemon
1½ lb. raspberries
3 lb. (6 cups) white sugar

Trim the rhubarb and cut into chunks. Place it in the cooking pan with the water, lemon juice and the lemon rind and pith tied loosely in a muslin bag. Bring to the boil slowly, simmer until the rhubarb is tender. Remove the muslin bag.

Inspect the raspberries, place them in a separate pan and heat very gently until the juice begins to come out.

Add the raspberries to the cooked rhubarb. Add the sugar and stir until dissolved. Bring to the boil and boil rapidly until setting point is reached (see page 12). Skim.

Pour the hot jam into hot clean jars. Cover.

Rhubarb Jelly

Rhubarb Jelly needs both acid and commercial pectin added. The flavour and set are much better, however, when the rhubarb is mixed with other selected fruits.

Rhubarb and Orange Jelly
3 lb. rhubarb stalks
8 fl. oz. (1 cup) water
4 large oranges
white sugar

Wash the rhubarb and chop roughly. Place it in the cooking pan with the water and the juice, grated rind and pith of the oranges. Bring to the boil and simmer until the rhubarb is very tender.

Pour the pulp and liquid into a jelly bag and allow the juice to strain through into a clean bowl, unaided. Do not press or squeeze the fruit.

Test for pectin (see page 11). Measure the juice and allow 1 lb. (2 cups) sugar for each pint ($2\frac{1}{2}$ cups) strained juice.

Place the juice and sugar in the clean cooking pan, stir until the sugar is dissolved. Bring to the boil and boil rapidly until setting point is reached (see page 12). Skim.

Pour the hot jelly into hot clean jars. Cover.

Rhubarb and Black currant Jelly
Make as for Rhubarb and Orange Jelly omitting the oranges and using $1\frac{1}{2}$ lb. rhubarb stalks and $1\frac{1}{2}$ lb. black currants. Cook each fruit in a separate pan, the rhubarb in $\frac{1}{4}$ pint ($\frac{5}{8}$ cup) water and the black currants with $\frac{3}{4}$ pint (scant 2 cups) water. Add the juice of 2 lemons to the rhubarb at the beginning of the cooking time. Strain the fruits together.

Rose Hip Jelly

2 lb. rose hips
2 lb. apples (prepared)
2 pints (5 cups) water
juice of 1 lemon
white sugar

Wash the rose hips and apples and chop the apples roughly. Place the fruit in separate cooking pans and add half the water to each. Add the lemon juice to the hips. Bring both pans gently to the boil then simmer until the fruit is soft and pulpy.

Making Marmalades

Place the juice and pulp together in a jelly bag and allow the juice to strain through into a clean bowl. Do not press or squeeze the fruit.

Test for pectin (see page 11). Measure the strained juice and allow 1 lb. (2 cups) sugar for each pint (2½ cups) juice.

Place the juice and sugar in the clean cooking pan. Bring to the boil, stirring until the sugar is dissolved, then boil rapidly until setting point is reached (see page 12). Skim.

Pour the hot jelly into clean hot jars. Cover.

Spiced Rose Hip Jelly

Make as for Rose Hip Jelly, but add a small

cinnamon stick and 6 cloves to the hips at the beginning of the cooking time.

Red Currant Jelly

6 lb. red currants
1 tablespoon (1¼T) water
white sugar

Wash the red currants and place them in the cooking pan with the water. Heat very gently and cook until the fruit is soft and tender. Mash the fruit well.

Pour the fruit and juice into a jelly bag and allow the juice to strain through without pressing or squeezing the fruit.

Test for pectin (see page 11). Measure the juice and allow 1¼ lb. (2½ cups) sugar for each pint (2½ cups) strained juice.

Place the juice and the sugar in the clean cooking pan, bring to the boil stirring constantly, then boil for 1 minute. Skim and pour into hot clean jars immediately. Cover.

Economical Red Currant Jelly
A less firmly set but easier red currant jelly can be made in the same way as Currant jelly (see page 23). The yield is also greater.

Strawberry Jam

This jam is notoriously difficult to make because strawberries are low in pectin and acid. The little there is, is in the skin and it is practically impossible to keep the fruit whole but at the same time extract the pectin. Additional pectin is usually supplied, either by using some fruit juice which is rich in pectin or by adding the juice, pith and rinds of lemons.

3½ lb. strawberries   Yields about 5 lb.
2 lemons
3 lb. (6 cups) white sugar

Hull the strawberries and place them in the cooking pan with the lemon juice and the lemon rind and pith tied in a muslin bag. Heat gently,

stirring, until the juice begins to run. Simmer until the fruit is tender and the contents of the pan reduced.

Add the sugar, stir until dissolved. Boil rapidly until setting point is reached (see page 12).

Skim the jam immediately then allow it to cool slightly before pouring into hot jars. Cover when cold.

Whole Fruit Strawberry Jam

3½ lb. strawberries
3 lb. (6 cups) white sugar
½ pint (1¼ cups) red currant juice

Place the hulled strawberries in the cooking pan with the sugar. Heat gently, stirring constantly,

2 lb. gooseberries
¾ pint (scant 2 cups) water
4 lb. (8 cups) white sugar

Hull the strawberries and top and tail the gooseberries. Place the fruit in separate pans and add the water to the gooseberries. Cook the strawberries over a low heat, stirring, until the juice begins to run. Bring the gooseberries to the boil and simmer until tender. Combine the two fruits.

Add the sugar, stir until dissolved. Bring to the boil and boil rapidly until setting point is reached (see page 12). Skim.

Pour the hot jam into hot clean jars. Cover.

Strawberry and Apple Jam

Make as for Strawberry and Gooseberry Jam (see above) using 2 lb. prepared apples instead of the gooseberries. Add the juice of 2 lemons to the apples at the beginning of the cooking time.

Strawberry Conserve

Make in the same way as Raspberry Conserve (see page 37), using the same quantities and ingredients, but substituting strawberries for raspberries.

Strawberry Jelly

Strawberries should either be used in equal quantities with another fruit that is acid and rich in pectin, like red currants, gooseberries or apples, or a commercial pectin must be added as directed on the packet.

Strawberry and Gooseberry Jelly
1½ lb. strawberries
1½ lb. gooseberries
½ pint (1¼ cups) water
white sugar

Wash both fruits and place them together in the cooking pan with the water. Bring to the boil then simmer until the fruit is soft and pulpy. Mash the fruit.

Place the pulp and juice in a jelly bag and allow the juice to strain through into a clean bowl. Do not press or squeeze the fruit.

Test for pectin (see page 11). Measure the juice and allow 1 lb. (2 cups) sugar for each pint (2½ cups) juice.

Place the strained juice and the sugar in the clean cooking pan. Bring to the boil, stirring until the sugar has dissolved then boil rapidly until setting point is reached (see page 12). Skim.

Pour the hot jelly into hot clean jars. Cover.

until the sugar is dissolved. Add the red currant juice and boil rapidly until setting point is reached (see page 12). Skim.

Cool slightly before pouring the jam into hot jars. Cover.

NOTE: Commercial pectin, used according to the directions given, can be used instead of red currant juice in this recipe.

Honeyed Strawberry Jam

Make as for Whole Fruit Strawberry Jam (see above). Stir in 4 oz. (good ½ cup) honey when the sugar has dissolved.

Strawberry and Gooseberry Jam

2 lb. strawberries   Yields about 7 lb.

Overleaf: Fig and Apple Jam

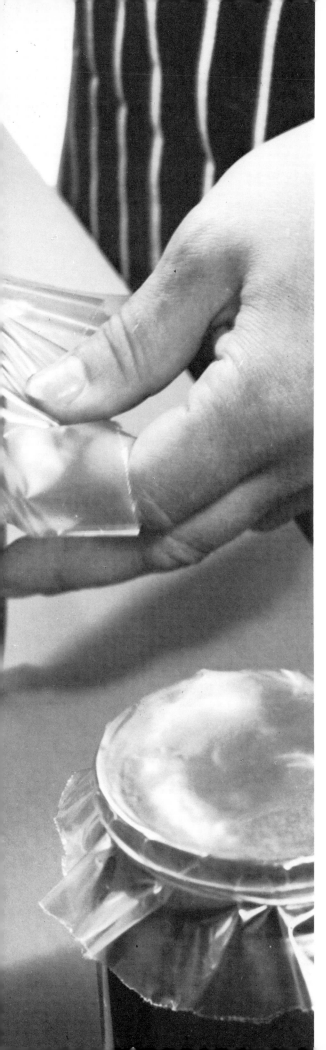

Strawberry and Red Currant Jelly
Make as for Strawberry and Gooseberry Jelly, using red currants in place of gooseberries.

Brandied Four Fruit Jam

8 oz. black currants   Yields about 5 lb.
8 oz. red currants
8 oz. cherries (9–10 oz. with stones)
8 oz. gooseberries
1 pint (2½ cups) water
3 lb. (6 cups) white sugar
3 tablespoons (3¾T) brandy

Remove the currants from the stems. Pit the cherries. Top and tail the gooseberries. Place the gooseberries in the cooking pan with the water. Bring to the boil and simmer for 15 minutes. Add the remaining fruit and continue cooking for about 30 minutes or until the fruit skins are tender. The contents of the pan should be thickening and well reduced.
Add the sugar, stir until dissolved. Stir in the brandy. Boil rapidly until setting point is reached (see page 12). Skim.
Pour the hot jam into hot clean jars. Cover.

Mixed Tropical Fruit Jam

1 lb. peaches   Yields about 5½ lb.
1 lb. apricots
½ lb. (2) nectarines
½ lb. diced (1 heaping cup) pineapple
3 passion fruit
3 bananas
3 lb. (6 cups) white sugar

Wash the fruit. Slice the peaches, apricots and nectarines, remove the stones. Chop the pineapple finely, reserving any juice. Scoop the seeds and pulp out of the passion fruit shells. Place all the prepared fruit and juice in the cooking pan, bring gently to the boil and simmer until the fruits are tender and the mixture is thickening, stirring occasionally.
Slice the bananas and add to the pan with the sugar. Stir until the sugar is dissolved then bring to the boil and boil rapidly until setting point is reached (see page 12). Skim.
Pour the hot jam into hot clean jars. Cover.

Fresh Fruit Jam

This jam is specifically for long-term storage in the food freezer; it will keep for 6 to 8 months. If you do not have a freezer but feel that the jam is worth making for its most delicious flavour, keep it in the refrigerator, but only for up to 4 weeks.

Covering Jars with Polythene

Fresh Raspberry Jam Yields about 4 lb.
1¼ pints (good 3 cups) crushed raspberries
2 lb. (5⅓ cups) castor (superfine) sugar
2 tablespoons (2½T) lemon juice
4 fl. oz. (½ cup) liquid commercial pectin

Place the crushed raspberries in a bowl and stir in the castor (superfine) sugar and lemon juice. Cover the bowl with a clean tea towel and put aside for at least 20 minutes or until the sugar is dissolved.
Add the liquid pectin and combine thoroughly, stir for 2 minutes. Ladle the jam into very clean jars or plastic containers. Cover the jars and seal airtight.
Allow the jam to stand at room temperature for 12–24 hours or until set then store (see page 47).

Fresh Red Currant Jam
Make the fresh raspberry jam as given above, substituting red currants for the raspberries.
NOTE: Most soft fruits can be made into fresh fruit jam using the above recipe; besides raspberries and red currants, strawberries are also very good.

Sugarless Jam

Sugarless jam is ideal for a diabetic diet. It has poor keeping qualities, however, as it is the sugar in ordinary jams that preserves them. Make only small amounts of this jam at one time.

1 lb. fruit
water
10 saccharine tablets or artificial liquid
  sweetener to taste
½ oz. (1 envelope unflavoured) gelatine

Inspect the fruit and wash, peel, core or remove the stones as required. Place it in the cooking pan with enough water to just cover. Bring to the boil and simmer until just tender. Cool.
Crush the saccharine tablets and dissolve them in 1 tablespoon (1¼T) hot water. Stir the sweetener into the cooked fruit.
Dissolve the gelatine in a little hot water and stir it into the fruit. Stir thoroughly.
Pour into hot clean jars and cover.
Store, when cool, in the refrigerator.

Lemon Marmalade

Limes can be used instead of lemons to make a delicious lime marmalade.

3 lb. lemons Yields about 10 lb.
6 pints (15 cups) water
6 lb. (12 cups) white sugar

Wash all the lemons thoroughly in warm water, remove the stalks. Cut them in half and squeeze out the juice. Remove the pips (seeds), cut away excess pith if it is very thick and tie the excess pith and pips (seeds) loosely in a muslin bag. Slice the skins into matchstick strips and place these in the cooking pan with the juice, pith and pips (seeds) and the water. Bring to the boil and simmer until the strips of skin are very tender. Remove the muslin bag and squeeze out any liquid.
Add the sugar, bring to the boil again, stirring until the sugar is dissolved. Boil rapidly until setting point is reached (see page 12). Skim.
Allow the marmalade to cool slightly before pouring it into hot clean jars. Cover.

Lemon Ginger Marmalade
Make as for Lemon Marmalade. Add 4 oz. chopped crystallized ginger at the same time as the sugar.

Spiced Lemon Marmalade
Make as for Lemon Marmalade. Place either 8 whole cloves or 1 stick cinnamon in the muslin bag with the pith and pips (seeds).

Seville Orange Marmalade

Seville oranges give this marmalade the best flavour. Other bitter oranges can be used if they are not available.

3 lb. Seville oranges Yields about 10 lb.
6 pints (15 cups) water
juice of 2 lemons
6 lb. (12 cups) white sugar

Remove the stalks and scrub the oranges very thoroughly in warm water. Cut the fruit in half, squeeze out the juice, remove the pips (seeds) and reserve them. Cut the peel into thin matchstick strips, remove excess pith if necessary and tie the pith and pips (seeds) loosely in a muslin bag.
Place the cut orange peel, juice and muslin bag of pith and pips (seeds) in the cooking pan with the water and lemon juice. Bring slowly to the boil, stirring occasionally, then reduce the heat and simmer gently until the peel is very tender, about 2 hours. Remove the muslin bag and squeeze out any liquid.
Add the sugar, bring to the boil, stirring until the sugar is dissolved. Boil rapidly until setting point is reached (see page 12). Skim.
Allow the marmalade to cool slightly before pouring it into hot clean jars. Cover.

Raspberry Jam and Red Currant Jelly For Freezing (left)
Cutting Peel into Matchstick Strips (overleaf)

Chunky Dark Marmalade
Make as for Seville Orange Marmalade. Chop the orange peel into chunks or put through a mincer, if time is short. Add 1 tablespoon ($1\frac{1}{4}$T) black treacle (dark molasses) with the sugar.

Grapefruit Marmalade

$2\frac{1}{4}$ lb. grapefruit   Yields about 10 lb.
3 lemons
6 pints (15 cups) water
6 lb. (12 cups) white sugar

Scrub the grapefruit and lemons throughly in warm water and remove the stalks. Cut the grapefruit in half, squeeze out the juice, remove the pips (seeds) and reserve them. Cut excess pith off the skins and put to one side. Cut the grapefruit skins into matchstick strips.
Cut the lemons in half and squeeze out the juice. Slice the lemon skins thinly and tie them loosely in a muslin bag with the lemon pips (seeds), grapefruit pips (seeds) and grapefruit pith.
Place the strips of grapefruit skin in the cooking pan with the grapefruit and lemon juices, the muslin bag and the water. Bring to the boil then reduce the heat and simmer until the grapefruit peel is tender, about 2 hours. Remove the muslin bag and squeeze out any liquid.
Add the sugar, bring to the boil again, stirring until the sugar is dissolved. Boil rapidly until setting point is reached (see page 12). Skim.
Allow the marmalade to cool slightly before pouring it into hot clean jars. Cover.

Grapefruit and Lemon Marmalade
Make as for Grapefruit Marmalade. Use 5 lemons instead of 3, cut the skins in matchstick strips and add them to the grapefruit strips in the cooking pan—do not tie them in the muslin bag.

Three Fruit Marmalade

The total weight of the three fruits should be about 3 lb.

2 grapefruit   Yields about 10 lb.
4 lemons
2 sweet oranges
6 pints (15 cups) water
6 lb. (12 cups) white sugar

Scrub all the fruit thoroughly in warm water and remove the stalks. Cut them in half, squeeze out the juices, remove and reserve the pips (seeds). Cut excess pith off the skins and slice them into thin matchstick strips. Tie the pips (seeds) and pith loosely in a muslin bag and place it in the cooking pan with the sliced fruit skins, the juices and the water. Bring to the boil then reduce the heat and simmer gently until the skins are tender, about 2 hours. Remove the muslin bag and squeeze out any liquid.
Add the sugar, bring to the boil again, stirring until the sugar is dissolved. Boil rapidly until setting point is reached (see page 12). Skim.
Allow the marmalade to cool slightly before pouring it into hot clean jars. Cover.

Sweet Orange Marmalade

The flavour of sweet oranges deteriorates during the long cooking so it is often advisable to add some flavouring.

3 lb. sweet oranges   Yields about $10\frac{1}{2}$ lb.
juice of 2 lemons
6 pints (15 cups) water
6 lb. (12 cups) white sugar

Scrub the oranges thoroughly in warm water, remove the stalks. Cut the oranges in half and squeeze out the juice. Remove the pips (seeds), cut off excess pith if it is very thick and tie the pips (seeds) and pith loosely in a muslin bag. Cut the peel into thin matchstick strips.
Place the cut up peel, juice, muslin bag of pith and pips (seeds) in a large bowl with the lemon juice and water. Leave to soak overnight.
Next day, place the contents of the bowl in the cooking pan. Bring to the boil and simmer until the peel is tender, about 1 hour. Remove the muslin bag.
Add the sugar, bring to the boil again, stirring until the sugar is dissolved. Boil rapidly until setting point is reached (see page 12). Skim.
Allow the marmalade to cool slightly before pouring it into hot clean jars. Cover.

Orange Coriander Marmalade
Make as for Sweet Orange Marmalade. Add $\frac{1}{2}$ tablespoon ($\frac{5}{8}$T) crushed coriander seeds to the pips (seeds) and pith in the muslin bag.

Brandied Orange Marmalade
Make as for Sweet Orange Marmalade. Add 2 tablespoons ($2\frac{1}{2}$T) brandy just before setting point is reached.

Tangerine Marmalade

Tangerines must be combined with other citrus fruit when making marmalade. The total weight of fruit for this recipe should be $2\frac{3}{4}$ lb.

tangerines   Yields about 5 lb.
1 small grapefruit
2 lemons
5 pints ($12\frac{1}{2}$ cups) water
3 lb. (6 cups) white sugar

Wash all the fruit very thoroughly in warm water, remove the stalks. Peel the tangerines, cut up the peel finely and tie it loosely in a muslin bag. Cut the grapefruit and lemons in half and squeeze out the juice. Chop the skins or mince them in a mincer. Tie the grapefruit and lemon skins, with pips (seeds), loosely in another muslin bag. Chop the tangerines and place them in the cooking pan with the bag of tangerine peel, the bag of lemon and grapefruit skins, the fruit juices and the water. Bring to the boil and simmer for 30 minutes. Remove the bag of tangerine peel and reserve. Continue cooking for a further 1½ hours. Remove and discard the muslin bag of lemon and grapefruit, squeezing out any liquid first.

Open the bag of tangerine peel and add the pieces to the cooking pan. Add the sugar, bring to the boil again, stirring until the sugar has dissolved. Boil rapidly until setting point is reached (see page 12). Skim.

Allow the marmalade to cool slightly before pouring it into hot clean jars. Cover.

Cumquat Marmalade

2 lb. cumquats   Yields about 5 lb.
¼ teaspoon salt
3 pints (7½ cups) water
juice of 1 lemon
white sugar

Wash the cumquats thoroughly in warm water. Place them in a bowl, cover them with boiling water and leave for 15 minutes. Then drain and dry them. Peel the cumquats, removing excess pith if necessary, then slice the peel very thinly. Slice the fruit, remove any pips (seeds) and place them in a small bowl with the pith and enough water to just cover. Leave overnight.

Next day place the cut up peel in the cooking pan with the salt and water. Bring to the boil and simmer until the peel is very tender, 1½–2 hours. Add the sliced fruit, the lemon juice and the strained liquid from the pips (seeds) and pith. Measure the whole mixture.

Return the mixture to the cooking pan, bring to the boil, reduce the heat and simmer gently for about 15 minutes.

Allow 1¼ lb. (2½ cups) sugar to each pint (2½ cups) of measured mixture. Add the sugar to the pan, bring to the boil, stirring until the sugar is dissolved. Boil rapidly until setting point is reached (see page 12). Skim.

Cool the marmalade slightly before pouring it into hot clean jars. Cover.

Jelly Marmalade

Orange Jelly Marmalade
                              Yields about 7½ lb.
3 lb. Seville or bitter oranges
6¼ pints (scant 17 cups) water
juice of 3 lemons
4½ lb. (9 cups white sugar

Wash the oranges, remove the stalks and place them in a large bowl. Pour on enough boiling water to cover them and leave for about 15 minutes. Drain and dry the oranges. Peel the fruit, remove any pith and cut the peel into fine shreds. Chop the remaining fruit roughly and place it with the pith in the cooking pan. Add 3¾ pints (scant 9½ cups) of the water and the lemon juice, bring to the boil and simmer, covered, for about 1½–2 hours. Place the shreds of orange peel in another pan with 1½ pints (3¾ cups) of water, cover the pan, bring to the boil and simmer for about 1–1½ hours or until the peel is very tender.

Strain the liquid from the peel into the cooked pulp. Reserve the shreds of peel. Place the liquid and pulp in a jelly bag and allow the juice to strain through into a clean bowl for 10–15 minutes. Return the pulp to the cooking pan and add the remaining 1½ pints (3¾ cups) of water, cover the pan, bring to the boil and simmer for a further 20 minutes. Return the pulp and liquid to the jelly bag and leave until all the juice has strained through. Do not squeeze or press the pulp in any way; leave overnight if necessary.

Pour the strained juice into a clean cooking pan, add the sugar. Bring to the boil, stirring until the sugar is dissolved. Stir in the shreds of orange peel. Boil rapidly until setting point is reached (see page 12). Skim immediately.

Allow the marmalade to cool slightly before pouring it into hot clean jars. Cover.

Grapefruit Jelly Marmalade
Make as for Orange Jelly Marmalade (see above), but instead of oranges and lemon juice use 3 grapefruit and 4 large lemons with a total weight of 3 lb. Do not include the lemon peel in the finished marmalade, cook it in with the rest of the fruit.

Three Fruit Jelly Marmalade
Make as for Orange Jelly Marmalade (see above), but instead of oranges and lemon juice use 3 grapefruit, 2 oranges and 3 lemons. The total weight of the fruit should be 3 lb.

Overleaf: Adding Sugar When Making Marmalade (left)
Pouring Marmalade into Jars (right)

Fruit Butters and Curds

There is a wide variety of preserves which are eaten in the same manner as jams, jellies and marmalade but are made in different ways. They have all been included in this chapter as they all look fairly similar.

Fruit Butters, Cheese and Paste

These are all basically the same mixture, they are just cooked to a different consistency and the amount of sugar used varies. The cooked fruit is rubbed through a fine sieve to make a pulp before sugar is added and the mixture is boiled rapidly until it has thickened. There is no setting test.

For fruit butter continue cooking until there is no free liquid and the imprint of the spoon can be seen in the mixture. The cold butter must hold its shape but be easily spreadable.

For fruit cheese the mixture should be so thick that if a spoon is drawn across the base of the pan it will leave a definite path. The mixture is put into small moulds and when served, unmoulded, it will hold its own shape and can be cut in slices or wedges. Smear the moulds with a very little glycerine before spooning in the hot cheese—this makes unmoulding easier.

Fruit pastes. The mixture is the same as that used for fruit cheese but the cooking is continued, stirring all the time, until almost dry. The cold mixture will be about the consistency of soft marzipan. Shape the paste into balls or oblongs and wrap in waxed paper to be served as confectionery.

Fruit butters and cheeses should be finished as for jam. Their keeping qualities are not so good, but can be assisted if the jars or moulds are covered with airtight lids.

Curds and Honeys

These are delicious preserves usually made from citrus fruits or passion fruit and thickened by cooking gently with sugar, butter and eggs. A honey is less stiff than a curd.

Honeys and curds should be cooked according to the recipe and completed as for jam. The keeping qualities are not good; they should be stored in a cool place and eaten within six weeks.

Previous page : Labelling Preserves (left)
A Selection of Marmalades (right)

Rhubarb and Orange Butter

4 lb. rhubarb stalks
4 oranges
water
white sugar

Wash the rhubarb well, chop it roughly. Peel the oranges thinly with a sharp knife or potato peeler, taking only the zest and none of the pith. Cut the oranges in half and squeeze out the juice. Place the rhubarb in the cooking pan with the peel and juice of the oranges. Add enough water to just cover the fruit. Bring to the boil, cover the pan and simmer until the rhubarb is very tender. Rub the pulp through a fine sieve. Weigh the purée and allow 8 oz. (1 cup) sugar for each pound (about 2 cups) purée.
Return the purée to the pan, bring to the boil and cook until it is beginning to thicken. Add the sugar, stir until dissolved. Bring to the boil and boil until no extra liquid remains, stirring occasionally. Pour into hot clean jars and cover immediately.

Damson Cheese

6 lb. damsons Yields about 7 lb.
½ pint (1¼ cups) water
white sugar

Wash the damsons and discard the stalks (stems). Place the damsons in the cooking pan with the water. Cover the pan, bring to the boil and simmer until the fruit is soft and pulpy. Rub the pulp through a fine sieve.
Weigh the purée and allow 1 lb. (2 cups) sugar to each pound (about 2 cups) of purée. Return the purée to the pan, bring to the boil again and boil, uncovered, until thickening. Add the sugar and continue cooking, stirring frequently, until very thick.
Pour into hot prepared moulds or jars and cover immediately.

Lemon Curd

Plum Gumbo

4 lb. plums   Yields about 7½ lb.
1 pint (2½ cups) water
2 oranges
1 lb. (3 cups) small seedless raisins
4 lb. (8 cups) white sugar

Wash the plums well and chop roughly, discarding the stones (pits). Place them in the cooking pan with the water, bring to the boil, cover the pan and simmer until soft and pulpy. Rub the pulp through a hair or nylon sieve.

Return the purée to the pan, bring to the boil and simmer until beginning to thicken. Peel the oranges and slice the fruit thinly, removing pips (seeds) and any pith. Add the orange slices to the pan with the raisins and sugar. Bring to the boil again, stirring until the sugar is dissolved. Boil until there is no excess liquid, stirring occasionally.

Pour into hot clean jars and cover immediately.

Apricot Butter

4 lb. apricots
juice of ½ lemon
water
white sugar

Wash the apricots thoroughly. Chop them roughly, discarding the stones (pits) and place in the cooking pan with the lemon juice and enough water to just cover them. Bring to the boil, cover the pan and simmer gently until the fruit is soft and pulpy. Rub the pulp through a fine sieve.

Weigh the pulp and allow 8 oz. (1 cup) sugar to each pound (about 2 cups) of apricot purée.

Return the purée to the pan, bring to the boil and simmer until thickening. Add the sugar, stir, until dissolved, bring to the boil and boil until there is no excess liquid, stirring occasionally.

Pour the hot butter into hot clean jars and cover immediately.

Spiced Apple Butter

6 lb. apples (windfalls or crab apples can be used)
2 pints (5 cups) water
2 pints (5 cups) cider
white sugar
1 teaspoon ground nutmeg
1 teaspoon ground cinnamon

Wash the apples thoroughly, remove the stalks and any bruised parts. Chop the fruit roughly, place it in the cooking pan with the water and cider. Bring to the boil, cover the pan and simmer until the apples are soft and pulpy. Rub the pulp through a fine sieve.

Weigh the sieved apple purée and allow 12 oz. (1½ cups) sugar for each pound (2 cups) of purée. Bring to the boil again and boil uncovered, until a thick creamy consistency. Add the sugar and the spices, return the mixture to the boil, stirring until the sugar is dissolved. Boil until there is no extra liquid left in the pan, stirring occasionally.

Pour the hot butter into hot clean jars and cover immediately.

Apple Ginger Butter

Make as for Spiced Apple Butter but instead of the cloves and cinnamon use 1½ teaspoons ground ginger.

Gooseberry Cheese

If the gooseberries are a little dull in flavour, try using dark brown soft sugar instead of white.

gooseberries
water
white sugar

Wash the gooseberries and place them in the cooking pan with enough water to just cover them. Bring to the boil, cover the pan and simmer until the fruit is very soft and pulpy. Rub the fruit through a fine sieve.

Weigh the purée and allow 1 lb. (2 cups) sugar for each pound (about 2 cups) of purée.

Return the purée to the pan, bring to the boil and boil, uncovered, until thickening and creamy. Add the sugar, stir until dissolved, continue cooking until very thick, stirring frequently. A spoon drawn across the base of the pan will leave a definite clean line.

Pour into hot prepared moulds (see page 58) or jars and cover.

Grape Cheese

Make in the same way as Gooseberry Cheese, (see above) using grapes instead of gooseberries.

Peach Cheese

Make in the same way as Gooseberry Cheese (see above) using peaches instead of gooseberries and adding the juice of 2 lemons to the cooking water.

Lemon Curd

4 lemons   Yields about 2 lb.
1 lb. (2 cups) white sugar
5 eggs
4 oz. ($\frac{1}{2}$ cup) butter

Scrub the lemons thoroughly in warm water and remove the stalks. Grate the lemon rinds finely, cut the fruit in half and squeeze out the juice. Place the rind in a large bowl with the juice, sugar, beaten and strained eggs, and the butter cut into small pieces.
Place the bowl over a saucepan of boiling water, making sure that it does not actually touch the water. Cook the mixture, stirring occasionally, until it begins to thicken.
Pour into warmed jars and cover immediately.

Orange Curd
Make as for Lemon Curd omitting the lemons and using instead 4 oranges.

Grapefruit Curd
Make as for Lemon Curd omitting the lemons and using instead 3 large grapefruit.

Tangerine Curd
Make as for Lemon Curd, omitting the lemons and using instead 10 tangerines and the juice of 2 lemons.

Mincemeat

There is a great variety of recipes for mincemeat. This one is both economical and tastes good. The alcohol can be omitted if preferred but this will drastically reduce the mincemeat's keeping time from about 1 year to about 2–3 weeks. Use firm cooking apples; juicy fruit will make the mixture too moist.

1 lb. cooking apples (peeled and cored)
8 oz. suet, shredded
12 oz. (2$\frac{1}{2}$ cups) seedless raisins
8 oz. (good 1$\frac{1}{2}$ cups) sultanas
8 oz. (good 1$\frac{1}{2}$ cups) currants
8 oz. (1 cup) mixed chopped peel
12 oz. (2 cups) soft brown sugar
1 lemon
1 orange
$\frac{1}{2}$ teaspoon ground mixed spice
$\frac{1}{4}$ teaspoon ground nutmeg
$\frac{1}{4}$ pint ($\frac{5}{8}$ cup) brandy or whisky

Peel and core the apples and chop finely. Shred the suet. Wash and dry the raisins, sultanas and currants. Place the prepared ingredients, and the shredded suet, in a large bowl with the chopped peel, brown sugar, grated lemon and orange rinds, juice of the orange and lemon and the spices. Stir well. Add half the brandy or whisky, stir well.
Pack the mincemeat loosely into clean dry jars and spoon the remaining spirits over the top. Seal.

Passion Fruit Honey

4 eggs   Yields about 3$\frac{3}{4}$ lb.
1 lb. (2 cups) white sugar
12 passion fruit
juice of 4 lemons
8 oz. (1 cup) butter

Beat the eggs and strain them into a heatproof bowl. Add the sugar and mix thoroughly. Cut the passion fruit in half, scoop out the pulp and add to the eggs and sugar with the lemon juice. Place the bowl over a saucepan of simmering water, making sure that the bottom of the bowl does not actually touch the water. Cook, stirring very frequently, until the mixture begins to thicken. Cut the butter into small pieces and stir into the "honey" until thoroughly combined. Pour into hot clean jars and cover.

Serving Mincemeat and Lemon Curd

Fruit Drinks

The best fruits to use for making into fruit syrup are damsons, black cherries, black and red currants, strawberries, raspberries and loganberries. Rose hips make a classic fruit syrup and the recipe for it follows this one as the method is different.

Fruit Syrup

fruit (see above)
water if necessary
sugar

Inspect the fruit, discard any that is bad or under ripe and wash if dirty. Drain well. Place the fruit in a large bowl and place it over a saucepan of simmering water. If currants are being used, add ½ pint (1¼ cups) water for each pound; blackberries will need ½ pint (1¼ cups) water for each 6 lb. The other fruits need no water.

Keep the water in the saucepan simmering all the time, adding more boiling water if necessary. Cook the fruit until the juices begin to flow. This will probably take about 1 hour. Press the fruit occasionally with a wooden spoon to help extract the juice.

Pour the pulp and juice into a jelly bag and allow the juice to strain through overnight into a bowl. Squeeze the bag hard to extract as much as possible. If you have a fruit press or juice extractor attachment for the electric food mixer, use these as they are more efficient than a jelly bag for extracting the juice.

Measure the juice and pour it back into the bowl with 12 oz. (1½ cups) white sugar for each pint (2½ cups) juice. Stir the juice until all the sugar is dissolved, without heating.

Pour the syrup into clean bottles and seal. Screw-top bottles are ideal but ordinary bottles and corks can be used if the corks are tied down firmly. The syrup should come to about 1 inch or less below a screw-top and 1½ inches below a cork. Place the bottles upright in a deep pan with a false bottom and support them with strips of newspaper. Add enough boiling water to come above the level of the syrup. Maintain the water at simmering point for 20 minutes. Remove the bottles from the water, screw down the tops or press the corks in again firmly.

NOTE: The corks and screw stoppers should be placed in a small saucepan with boiling water to cover and boiled for 15 minutes before using. Make sure they stay under the water all the time.

It is essential that the seal on the bottles is airtight if the syrup is to be kept for any length of time. When cold and dry, dip the cork-sealed bottles in melted paraffin wax to cover the neck of the bottle by ½ inch.

Rose Hip Syrup

This syrup is extremely rich in vitamin C. Two teaspoons each day will supply all you need. It makes an ideal addition to babies' and children's diets.

3 lb. rose hips
6½ pints (16¼ cups) water
1½ lb. (3 cups) white sugar

Mince the rose hips coarsely and place them immediately into a saucepan with 4½ pints (11¼ cups) of the water. Bring to the boil again then remove from the heat. Cover the pan and put aside for 15 minutes.

Pour the water and rose hips into a scalded jelly bag and allow the liquid to drip through into a clean bowl. Return the pulp to the saucepan, add the remaining 2 pints (5 cups) of water. Cover the pan and put it aside again for another 15 minutes. Strain the juice through the jelly bag as before.

Pour the strained juice into a clean saucepan, bring to the boil then boil until reduced to about 2¼–2½ pints (5½–6¼ cups). Add the sugar, stir until dissolved, and boil for a further 5 minutes. Pour the hot syrup into hot clean bottles and seal. Continue as for other fruit syrups (see above) except that the bottles should be processed in the hot water bath by boiling for 5 minutes not simmering for 20 minutes.

Lemon and Orange Squash

The flavour and colour of these drinks do not keep well so only make a little at a time and avoid storing them for longer than 2–3 months.

Lemon Squash
1 pint (2½ cups) pure lemon juice
3 lb. (6 cups) white sugar
1½ pints (3¼ cups) water
¼ oz. citric acid

Orange Squash
1 pint (2½ cups) pure orange juice
2½ lb. (5 cups) white sugar
1½ pints (3¾ cups) water
1 oz. citric acid

Wash the fruit thoroughly in warm water, scrubbing if necessary. Squeeze out the juice then peel the rind very finely, avoiding any of the pith (a potato peeler is good for this job).
Place the rind in a saucepan with the sugar and water. Heat the pan gently and stir until the sugar is dissolved. Strain the syrup through two thicknesses of muslin, into a bowl. Add the juice and citric acid. Mix thoroughly.
Pour the squash into clean bottles and seal.
Continue as for fruit syrups (see page 64). The bottles should be processed in the hot water bath by simmering for 20 minutes in exactly the same way.

Fruit Juices

Pure fruit juices can be extracted and processed in a hot water bath in the same way as fruit syrups (see page 64). The flavour deteriorates rapidly however if no sugar is added. Only 3 oz. (⅜ cup) white sugar need be added. Use the juices undiluted or with water and milk and some extra sugar.

Apple juice is the exception to the majority of juices as it needs no sugar. It is really only worth preparing however if you have a juice extractor attachment for an electric food mixer or a cider press. The apples should be washed in cold water and chopped finely before pressing. A second extraction can be made from the same apples by mixing the pulp with a little water—use ¼–½ pint (⅝–1¼ cups) to each 4 lb. apples. Sediment from the juice is also tricky to remove and the best method to use at home is to allow it to drip through a scalded jelly bag. The bag should not be pressed or squeezed but the juice be allowed to drip through unaided. The filling, sealing and processing of the bottles is as for fruit syrups (see page 64).

Trouble-shooting with fruit syrups, juices and squashes
Sediment in fruit syrups after storage:
(a) The strainer used was not fine enough. This is not detrimental to the flavour of the syrup.
Mould on the liquid or the cork:
(a) The processing time was not long enough.
(b) The water was not deep enough during processing.
(c) The cork was not boiled before using.
(d) The cork did not fit the bottle.

Tomato Juice (left)
Refreshing Summer
Fruit Juices (below)

Brandied and Candied Fruit

Brandying fruit is a good way of preserving those extra special, perfect fruits which would be spoiled if preserved by any other method.

The fruit is placed in the brandy and left there until thoroughly soaked. The skins of stoned fruits need to be pricked to allow the brandy to permeate the flesh and stop them from shrivelling. Seal the jars of fruit with plastic or plastic-coated metal covers.

Serve brandied fruit after a dinner party, with the coffee.

Brandied Grapes

grapes
sugar
brandy

Wash the grapes, if necessary, in gently running cold water. Drain and dry thoroughly. Separate the grapes into small bunches of two or three. Layer the grapes in a clean glass jar, sprinkling each layer with about 2 tablespoons ($2\frac{1}{2}$T) sugar. When the jar is full, pour over enough brandy to cover the grapes well.

Seal the jar and leave for at least 4 months before using.

Brandied Cherries

Prepare the cherries by cutting the stalks (stems) to $\frac{1}{2}$ inch from the fruit. Remove the stones (pits) carefully. Make the brandied cherries in the same way as Brandied Grapes.

Brandied Apricots

apricots
sugar
brandy

Wipe the apricots if necessary. Prick them to the stone all over with a silver hat pin or fine cocktail stick. Pack the apricots into clean dry jars with about 4 oz. ($\frac{1}{2}$ cup) white sugar for each pound of apricots. Pour in enough brandy to cover the fruit well.

Seal the jars and store in a cool dark place for at least 4 months before using.

Brandied Peaches

Prepare as for Brandied Apricots. The peaches may be cut in half if desired.

Brandied Cumquats

Prepare as for Brandied Apricots. Use 2 lb. (4 cups) white sugar to each pound of cumquats. Do not seal the bottles until the sugar is completely dissolved—it should take about 1 week if you stir the cumquats every day.

Candied Fruits

Candied fruits are very simple to make although the process is long and drawn out. If you can find the time to do it, the results can be rewarding and the cost only a fraction of what you would have to pay in the shops. Nearly any fruit can be candied although the stronger flavoured fruits are the most satisfactory—apricots, cherries, peaches, pineapple, plums. The peel of citrus fruits is also good. Both canned and fresh fruit can be used, but the process is slightly different so a recipe is given for each.

Use granulated white sugar for making the syrup or for an even better result use a proportion of glucose with the sugar. Do not mix the fruits when candying or the more dominant flavour will swamp the others. To improve the appearance of uninteresting-looking fruit, artificial food colouring can be added.

After the fruit is candied it can be finished with a glacé or crystallized appearance (see page 69).

Candied Canned Fruit

1 × 15 oz. can fruit (see above)
approx. 1 lb. 1 oz. ($2\frac{1}{8}$ cups) sugar or
13 oz. ($1\frac{5}{8}$ cups) sugar and 4 oz. ($\frac{1}{2}$ cup)
glucose

Open the can of fruit and strain the syrup into a measuring jug (cup). Place the fruit in a small heatproof bowl. Make the syrup up to $\frac{1}{2}$ pint

($1\frac{1}{4}$ cups) with water and pour it into a saucepan. Add 8 oz. (1 cup) sugar or 4 oz. ($\frac{1}{2}$ cup) sugar and 4 oz. ($\frac{1}{2}$ cup) glucose. Heat gently, stirring until the sugar is dissolved. Bring to the boil and pour over the fruit. Place a plate on top of the fruit to keep it completely immersed in the syrup. Cover the bowl with a clean tea towel and put aside for 24 hours.

Next day, strain the syrup into a saucepan, add 2 oz. ($\frac{1}{4}$ cup) sugar, heat gently, stirring until the sugar is dissolved. Bring to the boil and pour over the fruit. Cover the bowl and leave for 24 hours as before.

Repeat the above twice more, adding 2 oz. ($\frac{1}{4}$ cup) sugar each time.

On the next day (the fifth), strain the syrup into the saucepan, add 3 oz. (6T) sugar and heat gently, stirring until the sugar is dissolved. Add the fruit to the saucepan, bring to the boil and boil for about 3 minutes. Pour the syrup and fruit back into the bowl, cover as before and put aside for 2 days.

Repeat the above process, adding another 3 oz. (3T) sugar. At this point test the syrup for density; it should have the consistency of honey. Put a little of the hot syrup on a cold plate and allow it to cool, tilt the plate and you will be able to see the consistency of the syrup.

If the syrup is too thin, repeat the above process —adding another 3 oz. ($\frac{3}{8}$ cup) sugar—once more. Pour the fruit and syrup back into the bowl, cover as before and put aside for 3–4 days. If the fruit is not to be used straight away, leave it in the syrup, in a cool place for up to 3 weeks. Drain off the syrup, place the fruit on a rack (a grill pan or cake rack is ideal). Place the rack in a warm place such as a heated airing cupboard or the lowest setting of the oven with the door slightly ajar. The temperature should not exceed 120°F (50°C) or the fruit may brown and the flavour spoil. The drying process will take several hours and is complete when the fruit is no longer sticky. The fruit may be dried out of doors in sunny weather, but protect it from dust and insects.

Finish the candied fruit with a glacé or crystallized finish (see page 69).

Candied Fresh Fruit

1 lb. fruit (prepared)
approx. 1 lb. 2 oz. ($2\frac{1}{4}$ cups) sugar or
  14 oz. ($1\frac{3}{4}$ cups) sugar and 4 oz. ($\frac{1}{2}$ cup) glucose

Peel, core and halve or quarter the fruit or wash and remove the stone, depending on the type of fruit. Whole small fruit can be candied but the skins must be pricked with a silver fork or pin. Place the prepared fruit in a saucepan with enough boiling water to just cover. Bring to the boil again and simmer gently until the fruit is just tender. The time will depend on the size and variety of fruit. Over-cooking will result in an unattractive shape in the fruit; under-cooked fruit does not absorb the syrup readily.

Strain the cooking liquid into a measuring jug and measure $\frac{1}{2}$ pint ($1\frac{1}{4}$ cups). Place the fruit in a heatproof bowl. Pour the measured liquid into a saucepan, add 6 oz. ($\frac{3}{4}$ cup) sugar or 2 oz. ($\frac{1}{4}$ cup) sugar and 4 oz. ($\frac{1}{2}$ cup) glucose. Heat gently, stirring until the sugar is dissolved. Bring to the boil and pour over the fruit. Place a small plate on the fruit if necessary to keep it submerged in the syrup. Cover the bowl with a clean tea towel and put aside for 24 hours.

Strain the syrup into the saucepan again and add 2 oz. ($\frac{1}{4}$ cup) sugar. Heat gently, stirring until the sugar is dissolved. Bring to the boil and pour over the fruit again. Cover as before and put aside for another 24 hours.

Repeat the above process 5 times (adding 2 oz. ($\frac{1}{4}$ cup) sugar each time).

On the eighth day strain the syrup into the saucepan, add 3 oz. (3T) sugar. Heat gently, stirring until the sugar is dissolved. Add the fruit to the saucepan, bring to the boil and boil gently for about 3 minutes. Pour the syrup and fruit back into the bowl, cover as before and put aside for 2 days.

Repeat the above process once, adding another 3 oz. (3T) sugar. At this point test the syrup for density, it should have the consistency of honey. Put a little of the hot syrup on a hot plate and allow it to cool, tilt the plate and you will be able to see the consistency of the syrup.

If the syrup is too thin, repeat the above process, adding another 3 oz. (3T) sugar, until the required consistency is obtained.

Pour the fruit and syrup back into the bowl, cover as before and put aside for 3–4 days. The fruit can be kept in the syrup, in a cool place, for up to 3 weeks if necessary.

Drain off the syrup, place the fruit on a rack (such as a grill pan or cake rack) and put it in a warm place at a temperature of 120°F (50°C) to dry. The airing cupboard over the hot water tank, the plate rack of the cooker or the residual heat left after cooking in the oven is ideal. The drying will take several hours and the fruit is ready when it is no longer sticky to touch. The fruit may be dried outside in sunny weather but protect it carefully against dust and insects.

Finish the fruit with a glacé or crystallized finish.

Crystallized Finish

Dip the dried candied fruit quickly into boiling water with a skewer or fork. Drain off excess moisture then roll it in fine granulated or castor (superfine) sugar. Shake off excess sugar and store.

Glacé Finish

Only attempt a glacé finish if the atmosphere is dry. Humid atmospheres prevent the finish from drying.

Place 1 lb. (2 cups) white sugar in a saucepan with $\frac{1}{4}$ pint ($\frac{5}{8}$ cup) water. Heat gently, stirring until the sugar is dissolved. Bring to the boil, reduce the heat to keep the syrup hot and cover the pan tightly. Spear the fruit on a skewer or fork and dip it into boiling water for 20 minutes. Drain.

Pour a little of the hot syrup into a cup and dip the pieces of fruit into it, one at a time. Place the fruit on a wire rack. Continue until all the fruit has been dipped. Keep the bulk of the syrup hot in a tightly covered pan. The syrup in the cup needs to be changed whenever it becomes cloudy. Dry the dipped fruit, on the wire rack, in a temperature of 120°F (50°C).

Storing Candied Fruit

It is essential that the fruit is *not* stored in an airtight container as this encourages it to go mouldy. Simply use a wooden or cardboard box and separate the layers with waxed paper.

Candied Peel

2 oranges or lemons
water
4 oz. ($\frac{1}{2}$ cup) white sugar

Wash the fruit thoroughly in warm water, scrubbing if necessary. Score the peel into quarters and carefully remove it from the fruit. Place the peel in a saucepan with enough water to just cover. Bring to the boil, cover the pan and simmer gently for $1\frac{1}{2}$–2 hours or until the peel is very tender, adding more water if necessary.

Add the sugar, stir until dissolved then return to the boil. Remove the pan from the heat and allow it to cool, uncovered, until the next day.

Bring to the boil again and simmer for 2–3 minutes. Put the pan aside again until the next day.

On the third day, bring the syrup to the boil again and simmer gently until the peel has absorbed most of the syrup. Drain the peel and place it on a rack, pour any syrup that is left into the hollows. Dry as for candied fruit (see page 68).

Trouble-shooting with candied fruit

Sticky fruit after drying:

(a) The syrup was not sufficiently concentrated.

Sticky or mouldy fruit after storage:

(a) The packing was poor and the storage place damp.

Brandied Peaches (above)
Candied Fruit with a Crystallized Finish (right)

Vinegars

Making flavoured vinegars is a very individual matter—recipes vary greatly. There are, however, three rules which must be observed whether making flavoured vinegars or preparing a pickle or chutney in vinegar.

USE AN ENAMEL OR STAINLESS STEEL COOKING PAN. Aluminium pans can only be used if they are thoroughly scoured first.
USE A WOODEN SPOON. Reserve one spoon just for this purpose as it will absorb the flavour and may pass it on to other foods.
USE A HAIR, NYLON OR STAINLESS STEEL SIEVE, if one is needed for the recipe.

Spiced Vinegar

Spiced vinegar is used as the preserving agent in most pickles and chutneys. The vinegar used should be of the best quality available. Malt vinegar, whether brown or white distilled, has the best flavour and is usually more economical than other vinegars. White wine or cider vinegars can be used but the strong flavour of the pickle or chutney usually overpowers these delicate flavours. Use bottled vinegar with a reputable name; inferior bottled vinegars or those stored in barrels and bought in bulk are sometimes not suitable as there is insufficient acid in them. There must be at least 5% acetic acid.
The spices used in pickles and chutneys used to be added whole and were included in the finished pickle or chutney. This makes a less smooth flavour. Do not use ground spices as these cause a sediment to form at the bottom of the jar. Ideally, you should select the spices carefully according to the flavour you want your pickle or chutney to have and use them to flavour the vinegar before you start making the recipe. If you are planning to do a lot of pickling or chutney making, prepare the vinegar at the beginning of the season so that it is all ready.

2 pints (5 cups) malt vinegar
For a mild flavoured pickle:
  2-inches stick cinnamon
  12 cloves
  4 blades mace
  15 allspice
  8 peppercorns

For a hot pickle:
  2 tablespoons (2½T) mustard seed
  24 cloves
  24 black peppercorns
  2 tablespoons (2½T) allspice
  2 tablespoons (2½T) dried chillies

The amounts of the above ingredients can be varied according to taste. Additional flavourings you could add are crushed garlic, horseradish (scraped) and bruised root ginger. A ready mixed pickling spice can also be bought.
If you are planning ahead the best method of preparing the spiced vinegar is to add the spices to the bottle of cold vinegar and allow it to stand for 6–8 weeks, shaking the bottle occasionally. Strain before using.
If time is short, place the vinegar in a bowl over a saucepan of cold water. Cover the bowl with a plate. Bring the water to boiling then remove the pan from the heat and allow the spices to steep in the warm vinegar for about 2 hours. Strain, pour back into the bottle or use as required.

Flavoured Vinegars

Flavoured vinegars are ideal as a basis for interesting salad dressings as well as for some pickling.

Herbed Vinegar (Tarragon, Sage, Thyme or Marjoram)
2 pints (5 cups) white wine vinegar
4 oz. fresh herbs (see above)

Use the vinegar cold. Bruise the herb leaves and steep them in the vinegar in a tightly covered bottle or jar for 5–6 weeks.
Strain the vinegar and store in well sealed bottles.

Chilli Vinegar
2 pints (5 cups) white malt vinegar
100 chillies

Place the vinegar in an enamel saucepan. Cut the chillies in half. Bring the vinegar to the boil, add the chillies and boil for 1 minute. Pour into a hot jar, cover tightly and leave for at least 6 weeks.

Strain the vinegar and store in well sealed bottles.

Cucumber Vinegar
2 pints (5 cups) white malt or cider vinegar
10 small cucumbers
6 shallots
1 tablespoon (1¼T) salt
¼ teaspoon cayenne pepper

Place the vinegar in an enamel saucepan. Peel and chop the cucumbers and shallots, add them to the vinegar with the salt and cayenne pepper. Bring to the boil and simmer for 3–4 minutes. Place the vinegar and vegetables in a large jar, cover tightly and leave for at least 1 week.

Strain off the vinegar and pour into bottles. Seal well.

Onion Vinegar
2 pints (5 cups) malt vinegar
2 onions
1 tablespoon (1¼T) salt
1 tablespoon (1¼T) soft brown sugar

Place the vinegar in an enamel saucepan. Peel and chop the onions finely, add them to the pan with the salt. Bring to the boil and remove from the heat immediately. Pour the vinegar and onions into a large jar, cover tightly and leave for 2 weeks.

Strain the vinegar and store in well sealed bottles.

Celery Vinegar
Make as for onion vinegar using 1 large head of celery (well scrubbed) instead of the onions. Use white vinegar and granulated sugar.

Fruit Vinegars

Fruit vinegars are not so well known now as they used to be. They were once used to help cure sore throats, coughs and colds. Today, they can be served as a delicious and unusual accompaniment to steamed or baked puddings. Try them too when bottling fruit instead of a plain syrup.

1 lb. of fruit (soft fruit such as blackberries, mulberries, raspberries, black currants and elderberries are best)
1 pint (2½ cups) white wine vinegar
white sugar

Inspect the fruit and discard any bad pieces. Place in a china or glass bowl, add the vinegar

Chilli Vinegar in Preparation

and cover the bowl with a clean tea towel. Put aside for 3–5 days, stirring occasionally.

Strain the fruit. Measure the liquid and place it in a saucepan with 12 oz.–1 lb. (1½–2 cups) white sugar (according to taste) for each pint (2½ cups) liquid. Bring to the boil, stirring until the sugar is dissolved. Boil for 10 minutes.

Pour the hot fruit vinegar into hot bottles and seal.

Pickles

A pickle is one or more types of vegetable or fruit preserved in spiced vinegar. The vegetable or fruit keeps its shape and is recognizable in the finished preserve.

Choosing and Preparing the Vegetables or Fruit

Use only young fresh vegetables or perfect, just-ripe fruit. Cut the vegetables up into suitable sized pieces if necessary, cutting out and discarding any bad parts. Vegetables are usually soaked in brine or layered with dry cooking salt before bottling. Rinse off excess salt from the vegetables and drain thoroughly. Fruit is usually cooked in sweetened spiced vinegar before bottling. Prick the skins of whole fruit before cooking or they may shrivel.

Completing the Pickle

Pack the prepared vegetables or fruit into clean jars and add spiced vinegar, syrup or a prepared sauce to cover them by at least $\frac{1}{2}$ inch. The vegetables or fruit tend to absorb the liquid and those at the top may become exposed if they are not covered by this $\frac{1}{2}$ inch of liquid initially. Use cold vinegar unless a soft pickle is preferred, in which case you should pour boiling vinegar over the vegetables (making sure the jars are warm or they may crack).

Covering and Storing the Jars

Pickles should always be covered with an airtight cover. If the covers are not airtight the vinegar will evaporate very quickly. Plastic covers and plastic-coated metal caps are good, but take care not to use any plain metal caps as the vinegar will corrode them.

Label the jars and store them in a cool, dark place. Pickles should be kept for a short while for the flavours to mellow before being used. The exception to this is red cabbage which need only be kept for 1 week and will go soft if kept for longer than 3 months.

Trouble-shooting with pickles

Pickles shrunken in the jar:
(a) The covers were not airtight.
Cloudy vinegar:
(a) The vegetables were not left in the salt or brine for long enough.

(b) The vinegar was not strained through a fine enough strainer.
(c) Ground spices were used.
Spots on pickled onions after storage:
These are natural and not harmful; it is not known how they can be avoided.

Beetroot Pickle

beetroot (beets)
cooking salt
spiced vinegar (see page 72)

Wash the beetroot carefully so as not to damage the skins. Place it in a saucepan with boiling salted water to cover. Simmer, covered, for about $1\frac{1}{2}$ hours or until tender. Allow the beetroot to become completely cold then peel and slice it into $\frac{1}{4}$-inch rounds.

Pack the sliced beetroot (beets) into clean jars and cover with cold spiced vinegar, making sure it comes $\frac{1}{2}$ inch above the level of the beetroot (beets). Seal.

Sweet Beetroot Pickle

Make as for Beetroot Pickle (see above). Dissolve 1 teaspoon cooking salt and 4 oz. ($\frac{1}{2}$ cup) in each $\frac{1}{2}$ pint ($1\frac{1}{4}$ cups) hot spiced vinegar and allow it to become cold again before pouring onto the beetroot.

Beetroot and Onion Pickle

Make as for Beetroot Pickle (see above). Pack the sliced beetroot (beets) in layers alternately with slices of raw onion. Prepare the onion by placing the slices in a bowl and sprinkling with cooking salt. Cover the bowl with a clean tea towel and leave overnight. Drain, rinse and dry the slices before using.

Cauliflower Pickle

cauliflower
cooking salt
water
spiced vinegar (see page 72)

A Colourful Array of Pickles and Preserves

Wash the cauliflower and cut into flowerettes. Place in a large bowl. Make a brine using 8 oz. ($\frac{3}{4}$ cup) salt to 4 pints (10 cups) water and pour it over the cauliflower. Use a plate if necessary to keep the cauliflower under the brine. Cover with a clean tea towel and put aside for 24 hours. Drain the cauliflower thoroughly, pack it into clean jars and cover it with spiced vinegar. Seal. Leave for 14 days before using.

Sweet Cauliflower Pickle

Make as for Cauliflower Pickle (see above). Add 1 teaspoon sugar to each $\frac{1}{2}$ pint (1$\frac{1}{4}$ cups) vinegar several days before using it. Make sure the sugar is thoroughly dissolved.

Pickled Cherries

4 lb. Morello cherries
1 pint (2$\frac{1}{2}$ cups) white malt vinegar
2 lb. (4 cups) white sugar
4 cloves
1 inch root ginger
2 inches stick cinnamon

Stone the cherries, remove the stalks and wash. Drain.
Pour the vinegar into a saucepan with the sugar. Tie the cloves, ginger (bruised) and cinnamon in a muslin bag and add to the pan. Bring to the boil, stirring until the sugar is dissolved. Add the cherries, cover the saucepan and cook until the cherries are just tender.
Drain the cherries and return the vinegar to the saucepan. Pack the cherries into hot clean jars. Bring the vinegar to the boil again and boil, uncovered, until syrupy. Pour the strained hot vinegar over the cherries and seal. Keep any vinegar left over as the fruit tends to absorb liquid during keeping and the jars may need topping up.
NOTE: The stones may be left in the cherries if the look of the pickle is important.

Pickled Courgettes (Zucchini)

courgettes (zucchini)
cooking salt
water
spiced vinegar (see page 72)
dill seeds

Wash the courgettes (zucchini) and slice into $\frac{1}{4}$–$\frac{1}{2}$ inch rounds. Place the rounds in a bowl. Make a brine by dissolving 8 oz. (about $\frac{3}{4}$ cup) salt in each 4 pints (10 cups) water. Pour the brine over the courgettes (zucchini), cover the bowl with a clean tea towel and put aside for 24

hours.
Drain the courgettes (zucchini) and pack them into clean jars. Add enough cold spiced vinegar to cover the courgettes (zucchini) by $\frac{1}{2}$ inch. Place $\frac{1}{4}$ teaspoon dill seeds in each $\frac{1}{2}$ pint (1$\frac{1}{4}$ cup) capacity jar. Seal.

Pickled Cucumber

cucumbers
cooking salt
water
spiced vinegar (see page 72)

Wash the cucumbers and cut into slices or cut into quarters and then into shorter lengths. Place the cucumber in a bowl. Make a brine by dissolving 8 oz. (about $\frac{3}{4}$ cup) salt in each 4 pints (10 cups) water. Pour the brine over the cucumber, keeping it submerged with a plate. Cover with a clean tea towel and put aside for 24 hours. Drain the cucumber well and pack it into clean jars, cover with cold spiced vinegar. Seal.
Use after 1 week.

Sweet Cucumber Pickle

Make as for Pickled Cucumber (see above), but instead of spiced vinegar use white vinegar, mustard seeds and sugar. Use 1 tablespoon (1$\frac{1}{4}$T) mustard seeds and 1 tablespoon (1$\frac{1}{4}$T) sugar, to each pint (2$\frac{1}{2}$ cups) vinegar, place in a saucepan, bring to the boil and simmer for 5 minutes. Do not strain the vinegar.

Pickled Gherkins

Gherkins are small pickling cucumbers. Choose firm plump gherkins, not more than 2 inches in length, with the skin as smooth as possible.

gherkins
cooking salt
water
spiced vinegar (see page 72)

Wash the gherkins and place them in a bowl. Make a brine with 8 oz. salt (about $\frac{3}{4}$ cup) and 4 pints (10 cups) water, stirring well to dissolve the salt. Pour the brine over the gherkins to just cover them. Cover with a clean tea towel and put aside for 3 days.
Drain the gherkins and pack them into clean jars. Pour hot spiced vinegar over them, cover tightly and put aside for 24 hours, in a warm place.
Drain off the vinegar into a saucepan, bring to the boil and pour it over the gherkins again. Leave for 24 hours. Repeat this process until the gherkins are a bright green.

Cover with hot spiced vinegar and seal immediately.

Pickled Mushrooms

1 lb. button mushrooms
1 blade mace
6 white peppercorns
1 teaspoon salt
½ inch root ginger
½ small onion
white vinegar

Wipe the mushrooms with a damp cloth, using a little salt if they are very dirty. Place them in the cooking pan with the mace, peppercorns, salt, ginger and the onion. Add enough vinegar to just cover the mushrooms. Bring slowly to the boil, cover the pan and simmer gently until the mushrooms are beginning to shrink.
Pack the mushrooms into clean hot jars. Strain the vinegar, bring to the boil again and pour over the mushrooms. Seal.

Pickled Onions

pickling onions
cooking salt
water
spiced vinegar (see page 72)

Peel the onions, using a stainless steel knife to prevent discolouration. Place the onions in a bowl. Make a brine using 8 oz. (about ¾ cup) salt to 4 pints (10 cups) water; dissolve the salt thoroughly. Pour the brine over the onions to just cover them. Keep the onions under the brine by placing a plate on top of them. Cover the bowl with a clean tea towel and put aside for 24 to 36 hours.
Drain the onions thoroughly. Pack them into clean jars and cover with cold spiced vinegar. Seal.
Keep the onions for at least 3 months before using.

Pickled Red Cabbage

Choose a firm, good-coloured cabbage. Pickled red cabbage need only be kept for a week before it can be eaten but it should not be kept for longer than 3 months as it loses its crispness.

red cabbage
cooking salt
spiced vinegar (see page 72)

Trim the cabbage and remove the outer leaves. Shred the cabbage thinly and place it in a bowl in layers, sprinkling each layer liberally with salt.

Preparing Pears for Pickling

Adding Syrup to Pickled Pears

Packing Pickled Pears into Jars

Cover the bowl with a clean tea towel and put aside for 24 hours.
Drain off any liquid, rinse off any surplus salt and drain again. Pack the cabbage loosely into clean jars and cover with spiced vinegar. Seal.

Green Tomato Pickle

3 lb. green tomatoes   Yields about 6 lb.
1 lb. prepared marrow (vegetable marrow)
4 tablespoons (5T) cooking salt
2 small red peppers
3 cloves garlic, crushed
1 pint (2½ cups) brown malt vinegar
1 tablespoon (1¼T) dry mustard
1 teaspoon ground allspice
½ teaspoon each turmeric and celery seeds

A Dresser Full of Pickles and Preserves (left)
Chutneys and Pickles Made with Vegetables (below)

Pickling Vegetables (above)
Spiced Orange Slices (below right)

Wash and slice the tomatoes, peel and cut the marrow into ½ inch dice. Place the tomatoes and marrow in a bowl in layers, sprinkling each layer with salt. Cover the bowl with a clean tea towel and put aside overnight.

Next day, drain off any liquid and place the tomatoes and marrow in the cooking pan (see page 72). Wash the peppers, remove the seeds and membranes, chop finely and add them to the pan with the garlic. Blend the vinegar with the spices in a bowl then add this mixture to the cooking pan. Bring slowly to the boil then simmer, uncovered, stirring occasionally, until the vegetables are all very tender. This will take about 1 hour; the contents of the pan should be reduced and thickening.

Pour the hot pickle into hot clean jars and seal. Keep the pickle for at least 3 months before using.

Sweet Pickled Green Tomatoes

4 lb. small green tomatoes
cooking salt
13 fl. oz. (good 1½ cups) white malt vinegar
2¾ lb. (5½ cups) white sugar
water
2 teaspoons ground cinnamon

Wash the tomatoes. Make a brine in a saucepan with 1 oz. salt to each 4 pints (10 cups) water, bring to the boil. Put the tomatoes in the brine and simmer for 10 minutes, drain, rinse in cold water and remove the skins.

Place the vinegar, sugar and 6 fl. oz. (¾ cup) water in the cooking pan (see page 72) with the cinnamon. Add the tomatoes, bring to the boil and cook for 5 minutes. Pour the tomatoes and liquid into a bowl, cover with a clean tea towel and put aside for 1 week.

Strain off the liquid into the cooking pan, bring to the boil and boil for 10 minutes. Add the tomatoes and boil for a further 5 minutes.

Pack the tomatoes into hot clean jars and seal.

Piccalilli

There are two types of piccalilli, a hot one and a milder version. Use the sauce which you and your family will prefer.

2 cauliflowers
2 cucumbers
1 marrow (vegetable marrow)
2 lb. pickling onions or shallots
cooking salt
1 oz. allspice
2 pints (5 cups) white malt vinegar

Sauce 1 (Hot)
About 2½ tablespoons (3⅛T) turmeric (½ oz.)
About 6 tablespoons (7½T) dry mustard (1½ oz.)
About 7 tablespoons (8¾T) ground ginger (1½ oz.)
3 tablespoons (3¾T) plain flour (¾ oz.)
6 oz. (¾ cup) sugar

Sauce 2 (Mild)
About 2½ tablespoons (3⅛T) turmeric (½ oz.)
About 2 tablespoons (2½T) dry mustard (½ oz.)
1 teaspoon ground ginger
4 tablespoons (5T) plain flour (1 oz.)
6 oz. (¾ cup) white sugar

Wash the cauliflower and cut into small flowerettes. Peel the cucumber and cut into ½ inch cubes. Peel the marrow and remove the seeds, cut into ½ inch dice. Peel the onions. Place the prepared vegetables in a bowl in layers, sprinkling each layer with salt. Cover with a clean tea towel and put aside for 24 hours.

Rinse the vegetables and drain. Place the allspice in a saucepan with most of the vinegar, bring to the boil and boil for 2–3 minutes. Mix the sauce ingredients with the remaining vinegar to make a smooth paste. Strain the vinegar, stir it into the paste, return it to the saucepan and boil for 10–15 minutes, stirring frequently. Pour the sauce over the vegetables and stir to combine. Pack the vegetables into hot clean jars and seal immediately.

NOTE: The vegetables in this piccalilli are very crisp. For softer vegetables, add them to the sauce 5 minutes before the cooking time is completed.

Mixed Vegetable Pickle

1 cauliflower
1 cucumber
1 lb. French (green string) beans
8 oz. small pickling onions
cooking salt
spiced vinegar (see page 72)

Wash the cauliflower, drain and cut into small flowerettes. Peel the cucumber and cut into ½ inch dice. Wash the beans and cut into 1 inch lengths. Peel the onions.

Place the prepared vegetables in a bowl in layers and sprinkle each layer with salt. Cover the bowl with a clean tea towel and put aside for 48 hours. Wash the salt off the vegetables, drain them and pack loosely into clean jars, arranging the different vegetables attractively. Cover the vegetables with cold spiced vinegar and seal.

Clear Mixed Pickle

Make as for Mixed Vegetable Pickle (see above). Use white vinegar instead of malt vinegar. Cut a red chilli into strips, remove the seeds and salt with the rest of the vegetables. Add a strip of chilli to each jar when packing the vegetables.

Sweet Pickle and Apple

2 lb. apples (prepared)
2 cucumbers
4 onions
½ pint (1¼ cups) brown malt vinegar
8 oz. (1 cup) white sugar
1 teaspoon celery seed
½ teaspoon each ground ginger and turmeric
¼ teaspoon pepper

Peel, core and chop the apples. Peel the cucumber and cut into ¼ inch dice. Peel and chop the onions finely. Place the prepared apples and vegetables in the cooking pan (see page 72) with all the remaining ingredients. Bring to the boil, stirring until the sugar is dissolved. Reduce the heat and simmer for 30 minutes.

Pour the hot pickle into hot clean jars and seal immediately.

Pickled Walnuts

Walnuts for pickling must be very under-ripe. If the shell has begun to form they should be discarded. Prick the walnut at the stalk end with a needle; the shell forms about ¼ inch from the end.

walnuts
cooking salt
water
spiced vinegar (see page 72)

Wash the walnuts and place them in a large bowl. Make a brine by dissolving 8 oz. (about ¾ cup) salt in 4 pints (10 cups) water. Pour the brine over the walnuts, cover with a clean tea towel and put aside for 2–3 days. Drain the walnuts and cover with fresh brine. Put aside for 1 week.

Drain the walnuts and spread them out on shallow dishes or trays. Leave them for about one day or until they have gone black.

Pack the walnuts into clean jars and cover with spiced vinegar. Seal.

Leave for 1 month before using.

Sweet Walnut Pickle

Make as for Pickled Walnuts (see above). Use a sweet spiced vinegar. Place the following ingredients in a saucepan, bring to the boil and boil for 5–10 minutes. Strain and cool before using. 2 pints (5 cups) malt vinegar; 10 oz. (1⅔ cups) soft brown sugar; 1 teaspoon salt; 1 teaspoon peppercorns; 1 teaspoon allspice; 6 cloves.

Pickled Eggs

eggs
spiced vinegar (see page 72)

Place the unshelled eggs in a saucepan with cold water to cover. Bring to the boil, stirring the eggs gently to help keep the yolks in the centres. Boil for 15 minutes. Plunge the eggs immediately into cold water then shell them, removing the skin with the shell.

Pack the eggs into clean jars, cover with cold spiced vinegar and seal.

Keep for at least 1 week before using.

Pickled Apples

2 lb. small cooking apples
¾ pint (scant 2 cups) white distilled vinegar
1 lb. (2 cups) white sugar
8 cloves
2-inch stick cinnamon
8 allspice

Peel and core the apples and place them in a bowl with cold water to cover, to prevent them discolouring.

Pour the vinegar into a saucepan, add the sugar. Tie the cloves, cinnamon stick and allspice in a muslin bag and place it in the saucepan. Bring the vinegar to boiling point, stirring until the sugar is dissolved. Add the apples and simmer gently, covered, until they are just tender.

Pack the apples into hot clean jars. Bring the vinegar to the boil again and boil, uncovered, until syrupy. Strain the vinegar and pour it over the apples to completely cover. Keep any left over as the fruit absorbs more liquid on keeping and the jars may need topping up. Seal.

Keep for at least 6 weeks before using.

Pickled Crab Apples

Crab apples can be pickled in the same way as cooking apples, but need only to be cored, not peeled. Use brown malt vinegar instead of white and add 1 inch of bruised root ginger (ginger root) to the spices in the muslin bag.

Spiced Orange Slices

6 oranges
¾ pint (scant 2 cups) white malt vinegar
1 lb. (2 cups) white sugar
4 inches stick cinnamon
8 cloves
4 blades mace

Wash the oranges well in warm water. Place them in a saucepan with enough water to cover. Bring to the boil then cover the pan and simmer until the orange peel is tender. (The tines of a fork will pierce the peel easily). Drain the oranges and reserve the water. Cool the oranges quickly by plunging them into cold water and when cool, cut them into thin slices about $\frac{1}{8}$–$\frac{1}{4}$ inch thick.

Place the vinegar in a saucepan with the sugar and $\frac{1}{4}$–$\frac{1}{2}$ pint ($\frac{5}{8}$–$1\frac{1}{4}$ cups) reserved orange water. Tie the cinnamon, cloves and mace in a muslin bag and add it to the saucepan. Bring to the boil and simmer for 5–10 minutes. Add the orange slices, bring to the boil again and simmer for 30 minutes. Pour the contents of the saucepan into a bowl, cover it with a clean tea towel and put aside for 24 hours.

Next day, drain the orange slices and pack them neatly into hot clean jars. Remove the bag of spices and pour the syrup back into the saucepan. Bring the syrup to the boil and boil, uncovered, until thickening. Pour the syrup over the orange slices. Seal when cold.

Keep the spiced orange slices at least 6 weeks before using them.

Pickled Grapes

2 lb. Grapes
1 pint (2$\frac{1}{2}$ cups) water
$\frac{1}{2}$ pint (1$\frac{1}{4}$ cups) white malt vinegar
8 oz. (1 cup) white sugar
1 stick cinnamon
6 cloves
4 allspice
1 teaspoon crushed mustard seeds

Inspect the grapes carefully and wash if necessary. Pack the grapes into clean, dry jars.

Place the water, vinegar, sugar, cinnamon, cloves and allspice in the cooking pan. Bring to the boil, stirring until the sugar is dissolved. Remove from the heat, cover the pan and put aside for 1 hour.

Strain the syrup and pour it into the jars to cover the grapes. Add a few mustard seeds to each jar. Seal the pickle when cold.

Leave the grapes for at least 3 months before using.

Pickled Plums

4 lb. firm, ripe plums
2 pints (5 cups) malt vinegar
8 oz. (1$\frac{1}{3}$ cups) soft dark brown sugar
6 cloves
6 allspice
2 inches stick cinnamon
rind of $\frac{1}{2}$ lemon

Wash the plums and remove the stalks (stems). Place the vinegar and sugar in a saucepan. Tie the cloves, allspice, cinnamon and lemon rind in a muslin bag and add it to the saucepan. Bring to the boil and simmer for 20 minutes or until syrupy.

Place the plums in a bowl and pour the syrup over. Cover the bowl with a clean tea towel and put aside for 24 hours.

Next day, drain the plums and return the syrup to the saucepan. Reheat until boiling then pour the syrup over the plums again. Cover as before and put aside for 24 hours.

Next day, drain the plums and pack them into hot clean jars. Return the syrup to the saucepan, remove the bag of spices, reheat until boiling and pour it over the plums in the jars. Seal. Keep any extra syrup for topping up the jars as the fruit tends to absorb the liquid on keeping.

Quick Pickled Plums

For a quicker method of pickling plums, using the same ingredients as the previous recipe, add the washed plums to the simmering syrup the first time the ingredients are cooked together. Cover the pan and cook the plums gently until they are just tender. Pack them into hot clean jars. Return the syrup to the boil and boil until thickening. Pour the syrup over the plums in the jars and seal.

NOTE: The first method given is more laborious but the plums keep a better shape and it should be used when the look of the pickle is important.

Pickled Pears

Make the pickle using either of the two methods given for Pickled Plums (see above). Peel, core and cut the pears into eighths. Use white malt vinegar and white sugar for a clearer pickle.

Pickled Peaches

Make the pickle using either of the two methods given for Pickled Plums (see above). Plunge the peaches into boiling water for 30 seconds then rinse them in cold water to help remove the skins. Cut them into quarters or halves and remove the stones. Use white malt vinegar and white sugar for a clearer pickle.

Chutneys, Sauces and Ketchups

Chutney, sauces and ketchups are all basically the same mixture. For chutney the ingredients are cut up or minced finely, for sauces and ketchups, the ingredients are cooked and then sieved.

The flavour of all three depends largely on long slow cooking (usually at least 2 hours) and then the preserve is kept for a long period for the flavour to mellow. As long as all the bad parts are removed, any fruit or vegetables used in the recipes need not be in prime condition. Those fruit and vegetables which can not be preserved by other means can be used—chutney, sauces and ketchups are ideal to make when there is a glut of a certain fruit or vegetable.

Relishes
Relishes are a type of chutney and the recipes are included in this chapter because they are eaten in the same way, accompanying cold meat, salads and so on. The cooking time is not so long however and the finished preserve contains recognizable pieces of the ingredients.

Cooking chutneys, sauces and ketchups
The chutney ingredients should be finely chopped or minced so that the finished chutney is one thick mass, with none of the separate ingredients recognizable. Onions, garlic and other ingredients which need long cooking to tenderize them can, initially, be cooked separately in water in a small pan, as vinegar and sugar tend to harden rather than soften them. For sauces and ketchups, finely chopped ingredients will need less cooking and so save on time and fuel. The cooking must be very gentle and long; it is completed when all the excess liquid has evaporated and the mixture is thickened.

Completing the Process
Pour the hot preserve into very clean, warmed jars. Cover the jars when hot or leave them until cold before covering them. The covers should be airtight—plastic, or metal coated with plastic, is ideal. Home-made covers can be made by dipping cotton or linen pieces into paraffin wax. Label the sealed jars and store them in a cool dark place.

Keep the jars for at least 2 months before using. NOTE: Ripe tomato and mushroom sauces and ketchups need to be processed in a waterbath (as described in the recipes) otherwise they are liable to ferment with keeping.

Trouble-shooting with chutneys and sauces:
Separating of the vinegar:
(a) Undercooking.
Chutney shrunk in the jar:
(a) Covers not airtight.

Apple Chutney

7 lb. cooking apples   Yields about 10 lb.
1 lb. onions
1 oz. garlic (optional)
2 pints (5 cups) brown malt vinegar
3 lb. (8 cups) soft dark brown sugar
8 oz. crystallized ginger
1 lb. sultanas
1 teaspoon ground mixed spice
1 teaspoon cayenne pepper
1 teaspoon salt

Peel, core and chop the apples finely. Peel the onions and garlic and chop finely. Place the prepared apple in the cooking pan, (see page 72) with the onion, garlic and a little of the vinegar. Cook, covered, until the onion and garlic are very tender and the apple pulpy.
Add the sugar, spices and salt, with a little more vinegar if the mixture is very thick. Stir until boiling and then simmer, uncovered, stirring occasionally, for 15–20 minutes.
Add the remaining vinegar and continue cooking, stirring occasionally, until the chutney is thickened.
Pour into hot clean jars and seal when cold.

Sharp Apple Chutney

If a less sweet chutney is preferred, make the apple chutney as given above but reduce the amount of sugar used according to your taste. It can be omitted completely if liked.

Apple and Pear Chutney

Make the apple chutney as given above using 3½ lb. apples and 3½ lb. pears instead of all apples.

Apple and Banana Chutney

4 lb. apples   Yields about 10 lb.
12 bananas
1 lb. onions
8 oz. (good 1½ cups) seedless raisins
1 tablespoon (1¼T) salt
1 teaspoon each ground ginger, cinnamon
    and dry mustard
1 tablespoon (1¼T) curry powder
2 pints (5 cups) brown malt vinegar
1 lb. (2 cups) white sugar

Peel, core and chop the apples finely. Peel and slice the bananas thinly. Peel and chop the onions very finely. Place the prepared ingredients in the cooking pan (see page 72) with the raisins, salt and spices. Add half the vinegar, bring to the boil and simmer for about 30 minutes.

Add the remaining vinegar and the sugar, bring to the boil again, stirring until the sugar is dissolved. Continue simmering gently, stirring occasionally until the chutney is thickened.

Pour the hot chutney into hot clean jars. Seal when cold.

Apple and Date Chutney

2 lb. dates (stoned)   Yields about 8 lb.
2 lb. cooking apples
1½ lb. tomatoes
1½ lb. onions
1½ pints (3¾ cups) brown malt vinegar
12 oz. (2 cups) soft dark brown sugar
½ teaspoon ground cloves
½ teaspoon ground cinnamon
3 blades mace
½ teaspoon dry mustard

Chop the stoned dates finely. Peel, core and chop the apples finely. Plunge the tomatoes into a saucepan of boiling water for 1 minute then rinse them in cold water and remove the skins, chop. Peel and chop the onions very finely.

Place the prepared fruit and vegetables in the cooking pan (see page 72) with a little of the vinegar. Bring to the boil, cover the pan and simmer until all the fruit and vegetables are tender.

Add the remaining vinegar, sugar and spices. Bring to the boil, stirring, then cook, uncovered, stirring occasionally until the chutney is thickened, about 2 hours.

Pour into hot clean jars. Seal when cold.

Apple and Red Pepper Chutney

12 (sweet) red peppers
6 onions
2 lb. cooking apples (prepared)
½ pint (1¼ cups) brown malt vinegar
8 oz. (1⅓ cups) soft brown sugar
1 tablespoon (1¼T) salt
½ tablespoon (⅝T) celery seeds

Wash the peppers and chop finely, removing the membranes and seeds. Peel and chop the onions very finely. Place the prepared peppers and onion in the cooking pan (see page 72) with enough water to cover, bring to the boil then reduce the heat and simmer gently for 15 minutes.

Drain the peppers and onion, return to the cooking pan. Peel, core and chop the apples, add them to the cooking pan with the vinegar, sugar, salt and celery seeds. Bring to the boil, stirring until the sugar is dissolved. Simmer gently for about 3 minutes.

Pour the hot chutney into hot clean jars and seal immediately.

Apple and Tomato Chutney

3 lb. tomatoes
3 lb. apples
1 lb. onions
1 green pepper
8 oz. (good 1½ cups) sultanas
2 pints (5 cups) spiced vinegar (see page 72)
8 oz. (1⅓ cups) soft brown sugar
About 1 tablespoon (1¼T) salt (½ oz.)
¼ oz. root ginger, bruised
½ oz. (8–10 dry) red chillies

Skin the tomatoes by putting them in a saucepan of boiling water for 30 seconds then rinsing in cold water and removing the skins. Peel and core the apples, peel the onions, wash the pepper and remove the seeds and membranes. Chop all the prepared ingredients finely or mince them all together. Place them in the cooking pan (see page 72) with the sultanas, sugar, salt, ginger and chillies tied loosely in a muslin bag. Bring to the boil, stirring until the sugar is dissolved. Simmer gently, uncovered, stirring occasionally, until the vegetables are tender and the contents of the pan reduced and thickened. Remove the muslin bag.
Pour the hot chutney into hot clean jars and seal.

Apricot and Date Chutney

3 lb. apricots   Yields about 4½ lb.
1 lb. dates
1 lb. onions
1 lb. (2⅔ cups) soft brown sugar
1 tablespoon (1¼T) salt
1 teaspoon dry mustard
1 teaspoon turmeric
½ teaspoon each ground ginger and ground cinnamon
1¼ pints (good 3 cups) brown malt vinegar

Wash the apricots and chop the flesh finely. Remove the stones from the dates and chop finely. Peel and chop the onions very finely.
Place the prepared apricots, dates and onions in the cooking pan (see page 72) with all the remaining ingredients. Bring to the boil, stirring constantly. Simmer the chutney, uncovered, stirring occasionally, until it is thickened, about 2 hours.
Pour into hot clean jars. Seal.

Dried Apricot Chutney

8 oz. dried apricots   Yields about 3 lb.
12 oz. onions
8 oz. (1 cup) white sugar
1 orange
4 oz. (scant 1 cup) seedless raisins
1 teaspoon salt
1 clove garlic, crushed
1 tablespoon (1¼T) dry mustard
¼ teaspoon ground mixed spice
¾ pint (scant 2 cups) cider vinegar

Place the apricots in a bowl and cover them with cold water. Cover with a plate and put aside overnight.
Drain the apricots and chop them finely. Peel and chop the onions finely. Place the apricots and onions in the cooking pan (see page 72) with the sugar, grated rind and juice of the orange, raisins, salt, garlic, mustard, mixed spice and vinegar. Bring to the boil then simmer gently, uncovered, stirring frequently, until the contents of the pan are thickened. This will take about 1¼–1½ hours.
Pour the hot chutney into hot clean jars and seal immediately. Leave for at least 1 month before using.

Aubergine (Eggplant) and Pepper Relish

3 aubergines (eggplants)
2 (sweet) red peppers
2 cooking apples
4 onions
2 red chilli peppers
$\frac{1}{2}$ inch root ginger
1 tablespoon ($1\frac{1}{4}$T) coriander seeds
1 teaspoon salt
6 oz. (good 1 cup) sultanas
12 oz. (2 cups) soft brown sugar
1 pint ($2\frac{1}{2}$ cups) brown malt vinegar

Wash the aubergine (eggplant) and chop finely. Wash the red peppers, remove the seeds and membranes and chop finely. Peel, core and chop the apples finely; peel and chop the onions finely.

Wash the chilli peppers, chop roughly and tie them in a muslin bag with the bruised root ginger and the coriander seeds.

Place the peppers, apples and onions in the cooking pan (see page 72) with the muslin bag and the vinegar. Bring to the boil, cover the pan and simmer until the onions are tender. Add the aubergines (eggplants), salt, sultanas and sugar. Bring to the boil again, stirring, and simmer until thickened, stirring occasionally.

Remove the muslin bag and pour into hot clean jars. Seal.

Bengal Chutney

6 lb. cooking apples   Yields about $12\frac{1}{2}$ lb.
2 lb. onions
8 oz. preserved ginger (in syrup)
3 lb. sultanas (golden raisins)
1 tablespoon ($1\frac{1}{4}$T) salt
$\frac{1}{2}$ teaspoon cayenne pepper
4 oz. mustard seeds
2 oz. (about 20 dry) chillies
3 pints ($7\frac{1}{2}$ cups) brown malt vinegar
4 lb. ($10\frac{2}{3}$ cups) soft brown sugar

Peel and core the apples, chop finely. Peel and chop the onions very finely. Drain the ginger and chop finely.

Place the prepared apples, onions and ginger in the cooking pan (see page 72) with the sultanas, salt, cayenne pepper and the mustard seed and chillies tied together in a muslin bag. Add enough vinegar to just cover. Cover the pan, bring to the boil and simmer gently until all the ingredients are very soft.

Add the remaining vinegar to the pan with the sugar. Stir until the sugar is dissolved. Cook the chutney, uncovered, stirring occasionally, until thick. Remove the muslin bag. Pour the chutney into hot clean jars and seal.

Keep for at least 6 weeks before using.

Sweet Celery and Tomato Chutney

1 large head celery   Yields about 4 lb.
2 lb. ripe tomatoes
1 lb. onions
1 tablespoon ($1\frac{1}{4}$T) salt
8 oz. ($1\frac{1}{3}$ cups) soft brown sugar
$\frac{1}{4}$ teaspoon each ground allspice and nutmeg
$\frac{1}{2}$ teaspoon dry mustard
$1\frac{1}{2}$ pints ($3\frac{3}{4}$ cups) brown malt vinegar

Scrub the celery, discard the leaves and chop the stalks very finely. Skin the tomatoes by putting them in a saucepan of boiling water for 30 seconds then draining them and cooling under cold running water. The skins can then be easily slipped off. Slice the tomatoes finely. Peel and chop the onions very finely.

Place the prepared vegetables in the cooking pan (see page 72) with all the remaining ingredients. Bring gently to the boil, stirring, then simmer gently for $1\frac{1}{2}$–2 hours, stirring occasionally.

When the chutney has thickened and there is no excess liquid, pour it into clean warmed jars. Seal when cold.

Corn Relish

10 large cobs sweetcorn   Yields about 5 lb.
1 small cabbage
8 oz. (2 medium) onions
2 (sweet) green peppers
2 red chilli peppers
$\frac{1}{2}$ teaspoon celery salt
1 teaspoon dry mustard
$\frac{1}{4}$ teaspoon turmeric
2 teaspoons salt
1–$1\frac{1}{4}$ pints ($2\frac{1}{2}$–$2\frac{3}{4}$ cups) white malt vinegar

Place the corn in a saucepan of boiling water and cook for 5 minutes. Cool then remove the kernels and place them in the cooking pan (see page 72). Wash the cabbage and chop finely. Peel the onions and chop finely. Cut the peppers in half and remove the membranes and seeds, chop finely. Put the prepared vegetables in the pan with the corn, add the spices, salt and vinegar.

Bring to the boil and simmer until the corn is tender. Pour into hot clean jars and seal.

NOTE: The vegetables (other than the corn) can be minced; this is quicker and gives an equally good result.

Corn and Pear Relish

2 lb. corn kernels
½ white cabbage
2 pears
2 green peppers
1 red pepper
2 lb. (4 cups) white sugar
1½ pints (3¾ cups) white malt vinegar
1 teaspoon salt

Yields about 4½–5 lb.

Place the corn in the cooking pan (see page 72). Shred the cabbage finely, remove the seeds and membranes from the peppers and chop finely; peel, core and chop the pears. Place the prepared vegetables and pears in the pan with the corn and add all the remaining ingredients. Bring to the boil, stirring until the sugar is dissolved. Reduce the heat and simmer for 20 minutes. Pour the hot relish into hot clean jars and seal.

Cucumber and Tomato Relish

2 lb. cucumber (prepared)
2 teaspoons salt
2 lb. ripe tomatoes
1 (sweet) green pepper
1 (sweet) red pepper
1 lb. (2 large) onions
8 oz. (good 1½ cups) sultanas
1½ pints (3¾ cups) cider vinegar
1 lb. (2 cups) white sugar
1 teaspoon each curry powder and dry mustard
½ teaspoon each cayenne pepper, paprika pepper and ground ginger
2 tablespoons (2½ T) finely chopped mint

An Assortment of Preserves

Peel the cucumber and cut it into $\frac{1}{4}$ inch dice. Place it in a bowl and sprinkle with the salt. Plunge the tomatoes into a saucepan of boiling water for 30 seconds, rinse them in cold water and remove the skins. Chop them roughly. Wash the peppers, cut them in half and remove the seeds and membranes. Cut into $\frac{1}{4}$ inch dice. Peel and chop the onions very finely.

Put the vinegar into the cooking pan (see page 72) bring to the boil and stir in the spices. Drain the cucumber and add to the pan with the other prepared vegetables, the sultanas, mint and sugar. Stir until the sugar is dissolved.

Pour the hot relish into clean hot jars. Seal. Leave for at least 1 week before using.

Gooseberry Chutney

3 lb. gooseberries   Makes about 4 lb.
8 oz. onions
6 oz. (good 1 cup) sultanas
12 oz. ($1\frac{1}{2}$ cups) sugar
$\frac{1}{2}$ oz. mixed spice
1 teaspoon dry mustard
2 tablespoons ($2\frac{1}{2}$ T) salt
1 pint ($2\frac{1}{2}$ cups) malt vinegar

Top and tail the gooseberries and wash them. Peel the onions, chop them finely and put into a saucepan with enough cold water to cover. Bring to the boil and simmer the onions gently until tender, drain well.

Place the gooseberries in the cooking pan (see page 72) with the cooked onion and all the remaining ingredients. Bring to the boil, stirring continuously. Simmer, uncovered, stirring occasionally, until thickened.

Pour into hot clean jars. Seal when cold.

Lemon Chutney

6 thin-skinned lemons
1 lb. onions
4 oz. (scant 1 cup) raisins
$\frac{1}{2}$ teaspoon each dry mustard and ground ginger
1 teaspoon Tabasco sauce
1 teaspoon salt
1 pint ($2\frac{1}{2}$ cups) spiced brown malt vinegar (see page 72)
1 lb. (good 3 cups) soft brown sugar

Wash the lemons thoroughly in warm water and chop them finely, discarding the pips (seeds).

Making Gooseberry Chutney

Peel and chop the onions.

Place the lemons and onions in the cooking pan (see page 72) with the raisins, spices, Tabasco sauce, salt and ½ pint (1¼ cups) of the vinegar. Bring to the boil and simmer until the lemon rind is very tender. Add the remaining vinegar and the sugar. Bring to the boil again, stirring until the sugar is dissolved. Boil, uncovered, stirring occasionally, until thickened.

Pour into hot, clean jars and seal.

Orange Chutney

Make the chutney as given above using 5 thin-skinned oranges and 1 thin-skinned lemon instead of all lemons.

Mango Chutney

Mango chutney is the ideal accompaniment to a curry.

4 large mangoes
2 onions
2 oz. (½ cup) crystallized ginger
2 oz. (scant ½ cup) sultanas
8 oz. (1⅓ cups) soft brown sugar
1 tablespoon (1¼T) salt
¼ teaspoon each dry mustard and ground
  cloves
1 teaspoon ground ginger
½ teaspoon cayenne pepper
1¼ pints (good 3 cups) brown malt vinegar

Peel and slice the mangoes. Peel the onion and chop very finely.

Place the mangoes and onion in the cooking pan (see page 72) with all the remaining ingredients. Bring to the boil, stirring constantly. Simmer,

uncovered, stirring occasionally, until thickened, about 2 hours.

Pour into hot clean jars and seal.

Marrow Chutney

4 lb. marrow (vegetable marrow)
  (prepared)   Yields about 7 lb.
3 oz. (good ¼ cup) cooking salt
1½ lb. cooking apples (prepared)
1 lb. onions
8 oz. (good 1½ cups) sultanas
1 lb. (2 cups) white sugar
3 pints (7½ cups) malt vinegar
½ inch fresh root ginger
1 tablespoon (1¼T crushed dry) chillies
1 tablespoon (1¼T) peppercorns

Peel the marrow, chop into small pieces then place it in layers in a large bowl, sprinkling each layer with some of the salt. Cover the bowl with a clean towel and put aside overnight. Drain thoroughly.

Peel and core the apples and chop finely. Peel and chop the onion finely. Tie the ginger (bruised), chillies and peppercorns in a muslin bag. Place the prepared marrow in a cooking pan (see page 72) with the apple, onion and bag of spices. Heat gently then simmer, covered, until the vegetables are all very tender.

Add the sultanas, sugar and vinegar. Bring to the boil, stirring constantly. Cook until the chutney is thickened.

Remove and discard the bag of spices. Pour the chutney into hot, clean jars and seal.

Choko Chutney

Chokoes are pear-shaped vegetables that grow

wild in some countries. The flesh is very similar to that of a marrow and they could be used as a substitute in the above recipe.

Mint Relish

Makes about 2 pints (5 cups)

$\frac{3}{4}$ pint (scant 2 cups) cider vinegar
1 lb. (2 cups) white sugar
2 teaspoons dry mustard
1 lb. dessert apples (prepared)
2 onions
2 oz. (scant $\frac{1}{2}$ cup) seedless raisins
8 oz. fresh mint leaves
$\frac{1}{4}$ teaspoon salt

Place the vinegar in the cooking pan (see page 72) with the sugar and mustard. Bring to simmering, stirring until the sugar is dissolved. Remove the pan from the heat and allow to cool slightly.
Meanwhile, peel, core and dice the apples, peel and chop the onions very finely, wash the mint leaves and chop finely. Place the apples, onions and mint in a bowl with the raisins and salt. Pour on the hot vinegar mixture and stir to mix well.
Spoon the relish into hot clean jars and seal.

Pear and Ginger Chutney

4 lb. cooking pears   Yields about 6 lb.
8 oz. onions
1$\frac{1}{2}$ pints (3$\frac{3}{4}$ cups) brown malt vinegar
1$\frac{1}{2}$ lb. (3 cups) white sugar
6 oz. (1 cup chopped) preserved ginger
8 oz. (good 1$\frac{1}{2}$ cups) seedless raisins
$\frac{1}{2}$ teaspoon each ground mixed spice, dry mustard and ground cinnamon
1 teaspoon salt

Peel, core and chop the pears finely. Peel and chop the onions very finely. Place the prepared pears in the cooking pan (see page 72) with the onion and half of the vinegar. Bring to the boil and simmer until the pears and onion are very tender and pulpy.
Add the remaining vinegar, the sugar, the ginger (chopped), raisins, spices and salt. Stir until boiling and the sugar is dissolved. Simmer, stirring occasionally, uncovered, until the chutney is thickened.
Pour the hot chutney into hot clean jars. Seal when cold.

Plum Chutney

2 lb. cooking apples   Yields about 6 lb.
1 lb. onions
1 lb. (good $\frac{3}{4}$ cup) seedless raisins
3 lb. plums

1 pint (2$\frac{1}{2}$ cups) malt vinegar
1 teaspoon ground nutmeg
$\frac{1}{2}$ teaspoon each ground ginger, cayenne pepper and dry mustard
1 tablespoon (1$\frac{1}{4}$T) salt
1 tablespoon (1$\frac{1}{4}$T) allspice
4 cloves
6 oz. (1 cup) soft brown sugar

Peel and core the apples, chop roughly. Peel and chop the onions. Place the apples and onion in separate saucepans, add 1 tablespoon (1$\frac{1}{4}$T) water to each and simmer, covered, until soft and pulpy.
Chop the raisins, stone and chop the plums. Place raisins, plums, apples and onions in a cooking pan. Add $\frac{1}{2}$ pint (1$\frac{1}{4}$ cups) of the vinegar, the ground spices, salt, and the allspice and cloves, tied in a small muslin bag.
Bring to the boil, reduce the heat and simmer very gently, uncovered, stirring frequently, for 45 minutes.
Add the remaining vinegar and the sugar and continue cooking as before for a further 45 minutes to 1 hour or until thickened. Remove and discard the muslin bag.
Pour the hot chutney into hot dry jars. Seal when cold.

Red Pepper Jelly

This jelly is an ideal and unusual accompaniment to cold lamb, pork or poultry.

18 red peppers
cooking salt
2$\frac{1}{4}$ lb. (4$\frac{1}{2}$ cups) white sugar
12 fl. oz. (1$\frac{1}{2}$ cups) white wine vinegar

Wash the peppers, cut in halves and remove the seeds and membranes. Mince the peppers then place them in a bowl and sprinkle with salt. Put aside for 6 hours. Rinse the salt from the peppers. Drain well.
Place the prepared peppers in the cooking pan (see page 72) with the sugar and vinegar. Bring to the boil, stirring and cook, uncovered, for 30–40 minutes or until beginning to thicken.
Pour into hot clean jars and seal.

Rhubarb Chutney

3 lb. rhubarb   Yields about 3 lb.
12 oz. onion
4 oz. ($\frac{2}{3}$ cup) sultanas
1 lb. (2 cups) white sugar
3 teaspoons ground ginger
3 teaspoons salt
2 teaspoons curry powder
$\frac{3}{4}$ pint (scant 2 cups) white malt vinegar

Wash the rhubarb, trim and cut into small pieces. Peel and chop the onions very finely.

Place the rhubarb and onion in the cooking pan (see page 72) with the remaining ingredients. Bring to the boil, stirring constantly. Simmer gently, uncovered, stirring occasionally, until thickened.

Pour into hot clean jars. Seal.

Ripe Tomato Chutney

6 lb. ripe tomatoes   Yields about 4 lb.
8 oz. onions
1 pint (2½ cups) spiced white malt vinegar (see page 72)
2 teaspoons paprika pepper
¼ teaspoon cayenne pepper
About 1 tablespoon (1¼T) salt (½ oz.)
12 oz. (1½ cups) white sugar

Place the tomatoes in a pan of boiling water for 30 seconds. Drain, rinse under cold water and remove the skins. Chop roughly. Peel the onions and chop or mince finely.

Place the tomatoes and onions in the cooking pan (see page 72). Heat gently until simmering then continue cooking, stirring occasionally, until thick and pulpy. Add half the vinegar, the paprika pepper, cayenne pepper and salt. Bring to the boil and cook, uncovered, until thickened. Dissolve the sugar in the remaining vinegar, add to the pan and cook, stirring occasionally until thickened.

Pour into hot clean jars and seal.

Tomato, Apple and Raisin Chutney

4 lb. ripe tomatoes   Yields about 3½ lb.
1 lb. cooking apples
8 oz. onions
¼ pint (scant 2 cups) white malt vinegar
8 oz. (good 1½ cups) seedless raisins
1 tablespoon (1¼T) salt
¼ teaspoon each ground cinnamon, ground allspice, ground ginger, paprika pepper and cayenne pepper
12 oz. (1½ cups) white sugar

Place the tomatoes in a saucepan of boiling water for 30 seconds. Rinse them under cold water and remove the skins. Chop roughly. Peel, core and chop the apples. Peel and chop the onions.

Place the prepared vegetables and apples in the cooking pan (see page 72) with a little of the vinegar, the raisins, salt and ground spices. Heat gently until simmering then cook, uncovered, for 1½–1¾ hours. Dissolve the sugar in the

remaining vinegar, add to the pan and simmer until the chutney is thickened.

Pour into hot clean jars and seal.

Tomato Relish

3 lb. ripe tomatoes   Yields about 4 lb.
8 oz. onions
3 sticks celery
cooking salt
½ tablespoon (⅝T) curry powder
1 tablespoon (1¼T) plain flour
½ teaspoon dry mustard
1 pint (2½ cups) white malt vinegar
12 oz. (1½ cups) white sugar

Place the tomatoes in a saucepan with boiling water for 30 seconds, rinse in cold water and remove the skins. Chop the tomatoes roughly. Peel and chop the onion very finely. Wash the celery and chop finely. Place the prepared vegetables in a bowl and sprinkle them with salt. Cover the bowl with a clean towel and put aside for 24 hours.

Meanwhile mix the curry powder, flour and mustard in a bowl. Add enough of the vinegar to make a paste. Drain the vegetables, rinse off excess salt and place them in the cooking pan (see page 72). Heat gently until simmering then cook for 5 minutes. Dissolve the sugar in the remaining vinegar and add to the pan; simmer for about 30 minutes.

Add the flour paste and cook for 2–3 minutes, stirring constantly.

Pour into hot clean jars and seal.

Green Tomato Chutney

3 lb. green tomatoes   Yields about 6½ lb.
12 oz. onions
6 oz. (good cup) seedless raisins
12 oz. cooking apples (prepared)
2 tablespoons (2½T) salt
12 oz. (1½ cups) white sugar
1½ pints (3¾ cups) spiced vinegar (see page 72)

Wash the tomatoes and chop. Peel the onions, chop finely and place them in a saucepan with enough cold water to cover. Bring to the boil and cook the onions until they are tender, drain well. Chop the raisins if they are large. Peel, core and chop the apples finely.

Place the prepared fruit and vegetables in the cooking pan (see page 72) with the salt, sugar and vinegar. Bring to the boil, stirring constantly. Cook, uncovered, stirring occasionally, until thickened.

Pour into hot clean jars. Seal when cold.

Mushroom Ketchup

Makes about 1½ pints (3¾ cups)

3 lb. mushrooms (use large, mature mushrooms)
3 oz. (good ¼ cup) cooking salt
½ teaspoon blade mace
1 teaspoon allspice
1 teaspoon peppercorns
8 cloves
1 inch stick cinnamon
¼ oz. root ginger (1-inch piece ginger root), bruised
1 pint (2½ cups) brown malt vinegar

Wipe the mushrooms then break them into small pieces and place them in a bowl. Sprinkle the salt over them, cover the bowl with a clean tea towel and put aside overnight. Mash thoroughly.

Place the spices in the cooking pan (see page 72) with the vinegar and the prepared mushrooms. Bring to the boil then reduce the heat, cover the pan, and simmer for 30 minutes.

Strain the sauce through a fine sieve. Pour into hot clean bottles and seal at once.

Place the bottles in a deep saucepan with simmering water to come up to the neck. Keep the water simmering for 30 minutes, then remove the bottles.

Tomato Ketchup

4 lb. ripe tomatoes
cooking salt
2 onions
1 clove garlic, crushed
½ teaspoon blade mace
½ tablespoon (⅝T) white peppercorns
½ tablespoon (⅝T) allspice
¼ oz. root ginger (1-inch piece ginger root), bruised
1 bay leaf
¼ pint (⅝ cup) white malt vinegar
white sugar

Wash the tomatoes, drain and cut into thick slices. Place the tomatoes in layers in a bowl and sprinkle each layer with salt. Cover the bowl with a clean tea towel and put aside overnight.

Place the prepared tomatoes in the cooking pan (see page 72) with the peeled and chopped onion, garlic, spices and bay leaf. Bring gently to the boil, reduce the heat and simmer very gently, stirring occasionally, until thick and pulpy.

Rub the tomato pulp through a fine sieve and return to the rinsed cooking pan. Add the vinegar and sugar to taste. Bring to the boil

again and cook until beginning to thicken. Stir frequently.

Pour the ketchup into hot clean bottles and seal at once.

Place the bottles in a deep saucepan with simmering water to come up to the neck. Keep the water at simmering point for 30 minutes. Remove the bottles from the water.

Tomato Sauce

The redder the tomatoes used in this recipe the better the colour of the sauce will be.

Yields about 2½ pints (6¼ cups)

6 lb. ripe tomatoes
½ pint (1¼ cups) white malt vinegar
2 cinnamon sticks
1 teaspoon allspice
1 teaspoon blade mace
1 tablespoon (1¼T) salt
3 teaspoons paprika pepper
pinch cayenne pepper
2 tablespoons (2½T) tarragon vinegar
8 oz. (1 cup) white sugar

Wash the tomatoes and slice them thinly. Place in a saucepan and cook very gently until pulpy. Place the vinegar in the cooking pan (see page 72) with the cinnamon, allspice and mace. Bring to the boil then cover the pan and put aside for 2 hours. Strain the vinegar and return it to the pan.

Rub the tomato pulp through a fine sieve and return it to the saucepan with the salt, paprika pepper and cayenne pepper. Bring to the boil and simmer gently until thickening.

Add the tomato pulp to the spiced vinegar with the tarragon vinegar and sugar. Bring to the boil, stirring until the sugar is dissolved. Cook until the sauce is a thick creamy consistency.

Pour the hot sauce into hot clean bottles and seal at once.

Place the bottles in a deep saucepan with simmering water to come up to the necks. Keep the water at simmering point for 30 minutes. Remove the bottles from the water.

Green Tomato Sauce

Yields about 3 pints (7½ cups)

6 lb. green tomatoes
2 lb. apples
2 onions
1 lb. (2⅔ cups) soft brown sugar
½ teaspoon pepper
1 teaspoon dry mustard
2 tablespoons (2½T) salt
1 pint (2½ cups) spiced brown malt vinegar (see page 72)

An Assortment of Relishes, Chutneys and Jams (above right)
Making Pear and Ginger Chutney (below left)   Tomato Relish (below right)

Wash the tomatoes and apples and chop finely. Peel and chop the onions finely. Place the prepared tomatoes, apples and onions in the cooking pan (see page 72); add the rest of the ingredients. Bring slowly to the boil, stirring until the sugar is dissolved. Simmer gently, stirring occasionally, for about 1 hour.

Rub the sauce through a fine sieve. Return it to the rinsed cooking pan and bring to the boil again.

Pour the hot sauce into hot clean bottles and seal at once.

Blackberry Sauce

Yields about 1¾ pints (good 5 cups)

3 lb. blackberries
8 oz. apples
8 oz. onions
2 teaspoons ground ginger
1 pint (2½ cups) spiced vinegar (see page 72)
3 tablespoons (3¾T) salt
14 oz. (1¾ cups) white sugar

Inspect the blackberries carefully then place them in the cooking pan (see page 72). Wash and chop the apples. Peel and chop the onions. Add the apples and onion to the pan with the ginger and half the spiced vinegar. Bring to the boil and simmer gently, covered, until the ingredients are soft and pulpy.

Rub the sauce through a fine sieve and then return it to the rinsed pan. Add the remaining vinegar, salt and sugar. Bring to the boil, stirring until the sugar is dissolved. Simmer the sauce, stirring occasionally, until it is thickened and creamy.

Pour the hot sauce into hot clean bottles and seal at once.

Plum Sauce

Yields about 1¾ pints (good 5 cups)

4 lb. dark plums
8 oz. onions
4 oz. (scant 1 cup) sultanas (golden raisins)
2 teaspoons each allspice, peppercorns and mustard seeds
½ teaspoon cayenne pepper
¼ oz. root ginger (1-inch piece ginger root), bruised
1 pint (2½ cups) brown malt vinegar
2 tablespoons (2½T) salt
8 oz. (1⅓ cups) soft brown sugar

Wash the plums and chop them. Peel and chop the onions. Place the plums and onions in the

cooking pan (see page 72) with the sultanas, spices and half the vinegar. Bring to the boil then simmer gently for 30 minutes, or until the plums are soft and pulpy. Rub the contents of the pan through a fine sieve. Return the sauce to the rinsed pan. Add the remaining vinegar, salt and sugar. Bring to the boil, stirring until the sugar is dissolved. Simmer, stirring occasionally, for about 1 hour or until the sauce is beginning to thicken.

Pour the hot sauce into hot clean bottles and seal at once.

Horseradish Sauce

horseradish
cooking salt
white malt vinegar

Grate the horseradish finely. Make a mixture of 1 teaspoon salt to each pint (2½ cups) water and place the grated horseradish in this immediately to stop it from discolouring. After a few minutes, drain well and pack the horseradish into hot clean jars. Pour the vinegar into a saucepan, bring to the boil then pour it over the horseradish. Seal.

To use this concentrated horseradish sauce, place 1 tablespoon (1¼T) in a bowl and stir in ¼ pint (⅝ cup) cream and 1 teaspoon sugar.

Mint Sauce

If you have a lot of mint in the garden it can be preserved for the winter by one of the following methods and used as mint sauce. Use either method but don't mix them as the addition of both vinegar and syrup will cause the sauce to ferment.

Mint Sauce 1

Wash and dry the mint leaves thoroughly. Chop finely. Fill a small jar with chopped mint then cover with cold vinegar. Seal.

To use, spoon out as much concentrated mint sauce as required and add sugar and additional vinegar to taste.

Mint Sauce 2

Wash and dry the mint thoroughly and chop finely. Half fill a small jar with golden (light) syrup then stir in enough mint to completely fill the jar.

To use, spoon out as much of the concentrated sauce as required and add vinegar to taste.

Bottling Fruit and Vegetables

Nearly all fruits can be successfully preserved by bottling and it is an ideal way of keeping fruit throughout the year when there is a glut in season. Success in bottling, however, can vary with different varieties of the same fruit. The fruit is stored in syrup in jars which have been vacuum sealed, by heating, to prevent any mould or bacteria from entering the jar and spoiling the contents.

Choosing and Preparing the Fruit

Fruit for bottling must be ripe; under-ripe fruit lacks flavour and the colour is poor. Gooseberries are the exception to this rule as they are bottled green. All damaged parts must be very carefully removed or the fruit must be discarded. Besides being perfect, the fruit must also be clean and grease-free, so rinse it in cold water before using; it is not necessary to dry it. The most successful bottles of preserved fruit are made with fruit which is picked and processed on the same day.

Apples should be peeled and cored and then cut into $\frac{1}{8}$–$\frac{1}{4}$ inch rings, slices, quarters or halves. As they are prepared, place the apples into a bowl of salt water (1 tablespoon ($1\frac{1}{4}$T) salt to 2 pints (5 cups) water) to prevent them discolouring. When they are all prepared and just before processing, *either* pack the raw, rinsed apples into the jars *or* cook the apple, a little at a time, in boiling water until just tender. As a guide, the rings will only take 4–5 minutes. Pack the jars tightly as the apples tend to absorb some of the preserving syrup and sink down in the jars. Apples which are to be used for pie fillings can be bottled with other fruit as desired (blackberries for example). Try also bottling apples in a blackberry or lemon flavoured syrup. Alternatively, a delicious preserve can be made by adding a small piece of cinnamon stick or a few cloves to the jar, before processing.

Crab Apples should be peeled and cored and bottled whole. The flavourings suggested for apples can also be used.

Apricots can be bottled whole or in halves. The stalks (stems) should be removed and the fruit washed in cold water—it is not necessary to skin the apricots. The cut surface discolours quickly

so prepare halves immediately before processing. Some of the stones can be cracked, and the kernels removed and skinned, to be added to the bottles before processing.

Bananas can be bottled whole or cut into thick slices. Bananas discolour very quickly so prepare them immediately before processing. Add 1–2 tablespoons ($1\frac{1}{4}$–$2\frac{1}{2}$T) lemon juice to the syrup for each 2-pint (5 cup) capacity jar.

Bilberries (whortleberries, wineberries or blaeberries) make a delicious preserve. Use large berries which are well ripened. Pack the jar tightly, tapping it gently on the table occasionally.

Blackberries. Use early fruits, well ripened and plump but firm. Discard all the stalks (stems) and leaves, unsound and squashy berries; rinse the good berries in cold running water. Pack the jar tightly, tapping it gently on the table occasionally.

Cherries for bottling should be large, well ripened and firm. Remove the stalks (stems) and wash but leave the stones in. If it is essential that the stones be removed, carefully collect any juice and add it to the syrup. When a sweet variety of cherry is being bottled, the flavour is improved by adding 2 teaspoons lemon juice to each 4 pints (10 cups) syrup.

Chinese Gooseberries should be peeled and cut into slices $\frac{1}{8}$–$\frac{1}{4}$ inch thick.

Cranberries should be washed in cold running water and then soaked in a bowl of cold water for 2 hours before they are packed into jars. After filling the jar with syrup, leave the cranberries for 1 hour before processing. (This is to allow any air to rise to the surface).

Cumquats should be peeled and as much pith as possible removed. The fruit can be processed whole or cut into ¼-inch slices.

Currants (Black, red or white). Remove the stalks (stems) and rinse the currants in cold water. The calyx can be snipped off the black currants if desired. The jar should be very firmly packed; tap it gently on the table occasionally during packing, to push the fruit down. A few washed and bruised black currant leaves can be placed in the jar of black currants to improve the flavour. Red and white currants are good mixed with other fruit (for example raspberries).

Bottled Fruit (below)

Damsons need to be wiped free of all bloom and then rinsed in cold water. Remove the stalks (stems) and cut large fruit in half, removing the stones. Small damsons need to be stoned. Reserve any juice and add it to the syrup.

Figs need to be well ripened but still firm. Remove the stems and peel if liked. After the figs have been packed into the jars, add 1 tablespoon (1¼ T) lemon juice to each pint (2½ cups) capacity jar, then pour on the syrup.

Gooseberries are the only fruit which bottles more successfully when under-ripe and green. Each gooseberry should be snibbed ("topped

A selection of bottled fruit and jams (right)

GOLDEN PLUM

GOOSEBERRY

PEACH JAM

Storing Apricots for Bottling

Packing Apricot Halves into Jars

and tailed") before bottling and the skin pricked at least twice. Wash the fruit, if dirty, in cold water. Drain. Tap the jar gently on the table occasionally during packing.

Grapes should be picked from the stalks (stems). Rinse in cold water only if absolutely necessary.

Grapefruit should be peeled, the pith removed and the flesh cut into segments. Discard all the skin and remove all the pips (seeds).

Lemons are not the ideal fruit for bottling as they become cloudy with storage. They can be prepared, however, as for grapefruit or the juice alone can be processed.

Loganberries bottle very well indeed. Care should be taken initially to inspect the fruit and discard any berries that are squashy and bad, also any with maggots. Remove any leaves and the hulls.

Mulberries should be bottled when just ripe. Over-ripe and squashy fruit should be discarded. Handle the fruit as little as possible and process on the same day as picking.

Nectarines should be firm and ripe. Immerse the fruit in a saucepan of boiling water for 30 seconds then rinse in cold water and peel off the skin. These can be bottled whole but are more usually cut in half. Some stones can be cracked open and the kernels removed, blanched and returned to the jars with the syrup. Prepare the fruit just before bottling or it may discolour. Additional flavouring can be added to the fruit, besides the nutty kernels, by tying spices in a muslin bag and hanging the bag in the saucepan while making the syrup. For example, try adding 4 cloves, 1 inch cinnamon stick and 4 blades mace to each 4 pints (10 cups) syrup.

Oranges should be prepared in the same way as grapefruit.

Passion fruit. The pulp should be carefully scooped out of the skins directly into the jars. Do not add water or syrup to passion fruit before processing.

Peaches should be prepared in the same way as nectarines.

Pears come into two categories, cooking and dessert. Dessert pears are the most satisfactory to bottle. Peel, halve and core the pears and place them immediately in cold water with 2 tablespoons ($2\frac{1}{2}$T) salt and 2 tablespoons ($2\frac{1}{2}$T) lemon juice to each 2 pints (5 cups) water, to prevent discolouration. Pack the jars and process immediately. Cooking pears should be cut into quarters or sliced and poached in a syrup of 4 oz. ($\frac{1}{2}$ cup) white (superfine) sugar to 1 pint ($2\frac{1}{2}$ cups) water. The flavour can be improved by adding lemon peel, cloves or bruised root ginger (ginger root) to the syrup while cooking the pears.

Pineapple needs to be peeled, the hard core removed and the flesh cut into cubes or rings.

Plums can be bottled whole or can be halved if they are a free stone variety. Wipe off any bloom and prick the skin in various places to ensure that it doesn't split. Remove the stalks, rinse if necessary. Prepare halved plums immediately before processing as the flesh tends to discolour quickly. Some of the stones can be cracked and the kernels removed, blanched and added to the jars before processing.

Quinces should be prepared as for cooking pears.

Raspberries should be carefully inspected and any squashy or damaged fruit removed. If you suspect that there are maggots, spread the fruit in a single layer on a shallow dish and leave in a cool place for 1 hour. The maggots can then be removed as they will have emerged from the fruit. Rinse in cold water only if absolutely necessary.

Rhubarb needs only to be wiped with a damp cloth and then cut into the lengths desired. (It can be bottled at any length.) It can be packed into the jars raw. For a more economical method, soak the fruit in hot syrup—8 oz. (1 cup) white sugar to 1 pint (2½ cups) water—for 10 hours before packing. Use young bright red stalks of rhubarb for the best flavour. Additional flavouring can be given by peeling an orange, removing all the pith, slicing the flesh and adding it to the jar of rhubarb.

Strawberries tend to lose their colour when bottled and also they shrink in the bottle and rise to the top. To help get over these problems, after the strawberries have been inspected and the bad or squashy fruits removed, place them in a bowl, cover with syrup—8 oz. (1 cup) to 1 pint (2½ cups) water—and add a little red food colouring. Cover the bowl with a clean tea towel and leave overnight. Next day, drain the strawberries and pack them into the jars. Pour the syrup into a saucepan, bring to the boil and boil until there is 1 pint (2½ cups) liquid again. Use fresh syrup for the bottling process but add a little of the coloured syrup as well for added colour, about 2–3 tablespoons (2½–3¾T) to each pint (2½ cup) capacity jar.

Tomatoes can be bottled either in brine or in their own juices. Use well ripened firm tomatoes of even size and shape. Those processed in brine need only to be rinsed in cold water and the stalks (stems) removed. Tomatoes bottled in their own juices need to be skinned so dip them, a few at a time, into a saucepan of boiling water for about 10 seconds. Rinse them in cold water before peeling off the skin. Cut large tomatoes in halves or quarters and add 1 teaspoon salt and ½ teaspoon sugar to each pound of tomatoes. Pack the jars tightly.

Fruit pulp or Purée. Most fruit can also be made into a pulp or purée before processing if liked. All the bad parts must be removed from the fruit and it can be halved or sliced if desired. Place the fruit in a saucepan with just enough water to prevent it from burning; do not sweeten the fruit. Cover the pan and stew the fruit until tender—this will be anything from 15 minutes for soft fruit to 2 hours for cooking pears. The pulp can be sieved to make a purée and to remove any pips (seeds) from soft fruit, if liked, but the purée should be returned to a saucepan and brought to the boil again before being poured into the jars.

Making the Syrup
With the exception of tomatoes, most fruit can be satisfactorily bottled in syrup. Plain water

Pushing Fruit Well Down With a Wooden Spoon (left)   Adding Hot Syrup to Bottled Fruit (right)

can be used but the colour and flavour of the fruit deteriorate rapidly. The only drawback to using syrup is the appearance of the bottle of fruit as the fruit tends to rise to the surface if it is not very tightly packed initially.

The syrup most usually used is made of 8 oz. (1 cup) white sugar to 1 pint (2½ cups) water. Use granulated or loaf sugar for best results. Place the water and syrup in a saucepan and bring to the boil, stirring until the sugar is dissolved. Boil for 1 minute.

Very tightly packed fruit or fruit with a tart flavour might need more sugar. Adjust the syrup according to your personal taste.

Glucose or corn syrup, which are virtually tasteless, can be used instead of sugar for all fruits. Honey and golden (maple) syrup can also be used, but only with the stronger flavoured fruit such as black currants, gooseberries and rhubarb, as both these sweeteners have a strong flavour of their own. Use the same weights as given for sugar.

Saccharine should not be used as the fruit will become bitter. If sugar is not allowed, process the fruit in water and add the saccharine only when the fruit is used.

NOTE: The syrup should be clear, so strain it through several thicknesses of muslin if it is at all cloudy. For more luxurious and very delicious bottled fruits which can be used for desserts for special occasions, try adding liqueur to the syrup. After straining the syrup (if necessary) stir in ¼ pint (⅝ cup) liqueur to each pint (2½ cups) syrup. Choose the liqueur according to the fruit it is to flavour—for example, Grand Marnier with citrus fruit, Kirsch or Maraschino for cherries and plums. Unflavoured brandy is suitable for most fruit.

Choosing and Preparing the Jars

It is essential to use jars that can be sealed with a vacuum seal. It is not so much the jar that is important as the lid. There are two main types, those with a metal spring clip or those with a screw-band. Both sorts are used with a rubber sealing ring; these tend to stretch with use and it is advisable to use new ones each time to ensure a perfect seal. Soak them in warm water for 10 minutes then dip them in boiling water immediately before using.

There are special jars sold for bottling but it is also possible to use jam jars or even some coffee jars with metal lids, as seals are made for these by some manufacturers. For bottling in the pressure cooker, use only the special jars. The jars (whichever type you are using) must be free from any chipping or defects and scrupulously clean. If in doubt, sterilize the jars by placing

Pear and Apple Preserves

SPICED PEARS

PEAR + GINGER
CHUTNEY

BLACKBERRIES
WITH APPLE

them in a pan with a false bottom, covering them with cold water, bringing to the boil and continuing boiling for 5 minutes. Drain but do not dry the jars.

It is advisable to test the seal of the bottles and lids before starting. This can be done by filling the jars with water, putting the lids and seals in place and inverting the jars on the draining board. The leaking should stop after a few minutes.

Filling the Jars

Always fill the jars with as much fruit as can be fitted in without damaging or bruising. Don't just tip the fruit into the jar but carefully arrange it inside with the help of a long stick (the handle of a wooden spoon is quite good). Soft fruit should be filled into the jar until it is a third full; then tap the jar gently on the table before filling another third, tap again and fill to the top. Not only will this help to pack in as much fruit as possible but it will also help to remove any air that may be trapped between the fruit. (Place a cloth on the table first so as to avoid the possibility of cracking the jar.)

Whether the syrup is added hot or cold depends on the method you decide to use to process the fruits. Either way it is advisable to stand the jars on a tray to collect any spilt syrup. Hot jars should be placed on two or three thicknesses of newspaper.

Before adding the syrup, place the rubber sealing ring on the neck of the bottle (previously dipped in boiling water as described). The neck of the bottle must be very clean or the seal might not be complete. When the jars are filled with syrup, shake them very carefully to dislodge any trapped air bubbles. Top up the jars with extra syrup if necessary then put the lids and clips or screw bands in place.

NOTE: Screw bands should be tightened and then released for a quarter of a turn. This allows any build-up of steam to escape; if it is not done there is a danger that the bottle might explode.

Processing the Jars of Fruit

There are various methods of processing the fruit and they can be put into two categories. Choose the slow bottling method for best results but if time is scarce or you haven't a thermometer, the other methods give a good result for everyday use.

1. On top of the cooker (stove)—For this you need a large deep pan such as a saucepan or fish kettle. The pan must have a false bottom to stop the jars actually coming into contact with the hot base. A thick piece of newspaper, some thick cloth or a small rack can be used as a false bottom. The pan must be deep enough for the jars to be completely covered with water; or, if the water can only cover the shoulder of the jars (it must never come lower than this) the pan lid must be very tightly fitting to stop any steam escaping.

(a) Slow bottling—In addition to a processing pan you need a thermometer.

Place the cold, covered jars of fruit and syrup into the pan. Cover the jars with cold water and heat very gently. The water should be about 130°F (55°C) after 1 hour and the required temperature after $1\frac{1}{2}$ hours. Too rapid heating will cause the fruit to split. The required temperature should be carefully maintained.

(b) Quick bottling—Pack the fruit into warm jars and cover with hot (not boiling) syrup. Place the covered jars into the processing pan and cover them with warm water. Heat the pan until the water is simmering (not boiling) and maintain at simmering for the required time.

(c) Pressure cooker—If you have a pressure cooker, this is by far the quickest method of processing bottled fruit. The pan must be tall enough to take the jars and the 5 lb. weight (pressure) is used.

Pack the fruit into warm jars and pour in boiling syrup to come 1 inch from the top. Cover. Put at least 1 inch water into the pressure cooker then place a rack inside. Heat the pan until the water is simmering. Put the covered jars into the hot pressure cooker, put on the lid and heat until steam appears from the vent. Bring the cooker up to 5 lb. pressure slowly (this should not take less than 5 minutes, or more than 10). Maintain the pressure for the required time. Remove the pan from the heat and allow to cool for 10 minutes.

The processing temperatures and times for the various fruits are shown opposite.

2. In the Oven—for this you need a piece of cardboard, several thicknesses of newspaper or an asbestos mat to stand the jars on.

(a) Slow oven bottling—Pack the jars with the fruit but don't add any liquid. Cover the jars with lids but do not seal. Place the jars on a piece of cardboard and put them on the centre shelf of a very slow oven (250°F, Gas Mark $\frac{1}{2}$). The jars should be well spaced and away from the sides of the oven so that the air can circulate freely. The processing times depend on the fruit in the jars, how it is packed and the number of jars being processed at the same time. After processing, the jars should be carefully removed from the oven, one at a time, and immediately filled to the brim with boiling syrup. The rubber

FRUIT	SLOW BOTTLING	QUICK BOTTLING	PRESSURE COOKER
Apples (slices) Bananas Bilberries Blackberries Chinese Gooseberries Currants Gooseberries Loganberries Mulberries Passion fruit Raspberries Rhubarb Strawberries	Heat to 165°F (75°C) and maintain this temperature for 10 minutes.	Maintain at simmering (190°F, 88°C) for 2 minutes.	Maintain at 5 lb. pressure for 1 minute (NO LONGER)
Jars very tightly packed with the soft fruits listed above (except strawberries) Apricots (whole) Cherries (whole) Damsons (whole) Plums (whole) Cumquats Grapefruit Lemons Oranges	Heat to 180°F (83°C) and maintain this temperature for 15 minutes	Maintain at simmering (190°F, 88°C) for 10 minutes.	Maintain at 5 lb. pressure for 1 minute (NO LONGER)
Jars very tightly packed with the citrus fruits listed above apples (cooked) apricots (halves) nectarines peaches pineapples plums (halves) strawberries (soaked in syrup)	Heat to 180°F (83°C) and maintain this temperature for 15 minutes.	Maintain at simmering (190°F, 88°C) for 20 minutes.	Maintain at 5 lb. pressure for 3–4 minutes.
Figs Tomatoes (whole) Pears	Heat to 190°F (88°C) and maintain this temperature for 30 minutes.	Maintain at simmering (190°F, 88°C) for 40 minutes.	Maintain at 5 lb. pressure for 5 minutes.
Tomatoes (very tightly packed)	Heat to 190°F (88°C and maintain this temperature for 40 minutes.	Maintain at simmering (190°F, 88°C) for 50 minutes.	Maintain at 5 lb. pressure for 15 minutes.

FRUIT	SLOW OVEN	MODERATE OVEN
	Not recommended	
Apples (slices) Bananas Bilberries Blackberries Chinese Gooseberries Currants Gooseberries Loganberries Mulberries Passion fruit Raspberries Rhubarb Strawberries	When up to 4 one-pound jars (14 fl. oz. ($1\frac{3}{4}$ cup) capacity) are being processed: 45–55 minutes. When 5–10 one-pound jars: 60–75 minutes.	When up to 4 one-pound jars (14 fl. oz. ($1\frac{3}{4}$ cup) capacity) are being processed: 30–40 minutes. When 5–10 one-pound jars: 45–60 minutes.
Jars very tightly packed with the soft fruits listed above cherries (whole), black damsons (whole) plums (whole), dark apricots (whole)	When up to 4 one-pound jars are being processed: 55–70 minutes. When 5–10 one-pound jars: 75–90 minutes.	When up to 4 one-pound jars are being processed: 40–50 minutes. When 5–10 one-pound jars: 55–70 minutes.
cherries (white) plums (light coloured) cumquats grapefruit lemons oranges	Not recommended	
Jars very tightly packed with the citrus fruits listed above apples (cooked) apricots (halves) nectarines peaches pineapples plums (halves) strawberries (soaked in syrup)	Not recommended	When up to 4 one-pound jars are being processed: 50–60 minutes. When 5–10 one-pound jars: 65–80 minutes.
Figs Tomatoes (whole)	When up to 4 one-pound jars are being processed: 80–100 minutes. When 5–10 one-pound jars: 105–125 minutes.	When up to 4 one-pound jars are being processed: 60–70 minutes. When 5–10 one-pound jars: 75–90 minutes.
Pears	Not recommended	
Tomatoes (very tightly packed)	Not recommended	When up to 4 one-pound jars are being processed: 70–80 minutes. When 5–10 one-pound jars: 85–100 minutes.

A Colourful Array of Fruit and Vegetables for Preserving (above right)
Preserving Soft Fruits (below right)

sealing ring should be dipped in boiling water and placed on the neck of the jar before covering with the lid and sealing. Allow the jars to become cold before moving.

(b) Moderate oven bottling—Pack the jars with the fruit and pour in enough syrup to cover the fruit but to come 1 inch from the top of the jar. Cover the jars but do not seal. Process the jars in the centre of a slow oven (300°F, Gas Mark 1) as for slow oven bottling. Remove the jars and seal immediately.

Times for processing oven bottled fruit are shown on the table opposite.

Preparing Asparagus for Bottling

Cutting the Asparagus to fit the Jar

Tying the Asparagus in Bundles

Blanching the Asparagus

Packing the Asparagus into Jars

Covering the Jars

Putting the Jars into a Pressure Cooker

Storing the Sealed Jars

Leave the processed jars until completely cold—preferably the next day; then, before storing, test that the seal is good. Remove the spring clips or the screw bands and carefully lift each bottle by the lid. If the lid comes off, the jar must be re-processed or the contents eaten straight away. The screw bands may be replaced on the jars after testing but the spring clips should not as they could become weak and not be suitable for further use. Follow the manufacturer's instructions carefully when testing patent seals.

Store the jars of fruit in a cool, dark place.

Using the Fruit

Open the jars by inserting a knife carefully under the rubber ring and levering the lid off. Sweetened fruit can be used directly from the jar as a dessert. Unsweetened fruit is sometimes used for making jam. Unsweetened or sweetened fruit can be used for filling tarts, puddings and pies.

Trouble-shooting with bottled fruit
Jars not sealed:
(a) The rim of the jar, the lid or the rubber band were not perfect. This could be chipped glass or a small seed or piece of fruit might have become stuck under the lid.
(b) The sealing clip was not fitting or the screw band not tightened immediately after processing.
(c) Insufficient processing.

Fruit risen in the jar:
(a) The fruit was not packed into the jars tightly enough.
(b) The jars were processed too rapidly or for too long.

Bottled Asparagus

NOTE: Fruit bottled in syrup will nearly always rise a little and this is quite acceptable.
(c) Strawberries which rise have not usually been sufficiently soaked in syrup.

Mould on top of the fruit:
(a) Insufficient processing.
or fruit fermenting
(b) Inaccurate processing, e.g. jars not covered with water; too many jars in the oven; syrup not boiling when it should have been.
(c) The fruit was too ripe.

Fruit discoloured:
(a) Too long a delay between preparing the fruit and processing.
(b) The processing time was too long.
(c) The processing time was too short.
(d) Strawberries will nearly always have a bad colour when bottled unless artificial food colouring is added.

Syrup discoloured:
(a) The processing time was too long.
(b) The fruit was too ripe or was not cleaned.
(c) The syrup needed straining.

Bottling Vegetables

Like fruit, most vegetables bottle well; it is different varieties of the same vegetable that are processed with varying success. Some vegetables are easier than others to bottle and these are the

ones mentioned in this chapter. It is, generally speaking, only safe to bottle vegetables under pressure so it is unwise to attempt it unless you own a pressure cooker.

Choosing and Preparing the Vegetables
Use only vegetables which are in prime condition—this means in shape, flavour, colour and maturity. They should be graded so that a jar will contain vegetables which are as nearly identical as possible in size and colour.

The vegetables should be prepared and cleaned as you would do for eating. All blemishes should be removed and they should be scrupulously clean. Most vegetables need to be scalded before bottling. This means that they are immersed in boiling salted water for a short time then drained, dipped immediately in cold water and drained again. Each vegetable needs to be scalded for a different time. The following chart gives you the different times and some hints for preparing the vegetables:

VEGETABLE	PREPARATION NOTES	SCALDING TIME	PROCESSING TIME
Asparagus	Grade the stalks (stems) according to thickness. Tie in bundles for scalding—do not immerse the heads.	2 minutes thin stalks 4 minutes thick stalks	1 pint (2½ cups) capacity jars 30 minutes
Broad (Lima) Beans		3 minutes	35 minutes
French (string) or Runner (snap) Beans		2–3 minutes	35 minutes
Beetroot (beet)	Choose small beetroot (beets). Very small ones can be bottled whole, otherwise cut into ¼ inch slices or dice. Rub the skins off after scalding.	5–20 minutes	35 minutes
Broccoli	Divide into flowerettes and soak them in salted cold water for 24 hours. (1 teaspoon salt to 1 pint (2½ cups) water)	3–5 minutes	35 minutes
Brussels Sprouts		3 minutes	40 minutes
Carrots	Rub off the skin after scalding. Bottle whole or sliced. NOTE: Only young new carrots are worth bottling.	5–10 minutes	35 minutes
Cauliflower	Break into flowerettes. Add ½ teaspoon citric acid for each pint (2½ cups) water when scalding to help prevent discolouration.	3–5 minutes	35 minutes
Celery	Cut the cleaned celery to the height of the jar to be used. Add ½ teaspoon citric acid for each 2 pints (5 cups) water when scalding to help prevent discolouration.	3–5 minutes	35 minutes
Corn on the Cob	The cobs can be bottled whole or the grains can be removed from the cob and bottled separately, after scalding.	4–6 minutes	35 minutes
Courgettes (Zucchini)	Cut in half lengthways	1 minute	30 minutes
Leeks	Use young, thin stems and cut them to the height of the jar.	3 minutes	30 minutes

Mushrooms	(1) If the mushrooms are wide open, place them in a shallow dish, sprinkle with salt and pepper and cover with foil. Cook in a moderate oven (350°F, Mark 4) until the juice begins to run out. Pack the hot mushrooms in hot jars, cover with their juice.	None	30 minutes
	(2) Button mushrooms are best bottled in brine. After scalding, pack the mushrooms into the jars and pour over enough brine to cover. Use 3 oz. (about ¼ cup) cooking salt to 1 gallon (20 cups) water.	5 minutes	35 minutes
Peas	Up to 4 oz. (½ cup) white sugar can be added to each gallon (20 cups) brine if liked.	1–2 minutes	40 minutes
Peppers (Red and Green)	Place the peppers under a hot grill, turning occasionally until the skin is charred. Rinse the skin off under cold running water. Remove the seeds and membranes. Pack in layers. No liquid need be added.		40 minutes
Potatoes	Only new potatoes are worth bottling. Grade them to size. Rub the skin off after scalding.	5 minutes	40 minutes

Most of the vegetables not mentioned here are either not worth the trouble involved in bottling them or can be stored more satisfactorily by other methods. For 2 pint (5 cup) capacity jars, add another 5 minutes processing time.

Making the Brine

The brine should be made by heating the water and adding ½–1 oz. cooking salt for every 2 pints (5 cups). Stir to make sure that the salt is thoroughly dissolved. Always use it boiling and fill the jars full. A little green food colouring added to brine can improve the appearance of green vegetables (especially beans).

Choosing, Preparing and Filling the Jars

The choice and preparation of the jars are the same as for fruit bottling (see page 111). The jars must be robust enough not to break under 10 lb. pressure in the pressure cooker.

Fill the hot jars with the vegetables, packing them in carefully with the handle of a wooden spoon, but not so tightly that you squeeze them. Then pour the boiling brine over the packed vegetables until the jar is full. Cover the jars but do not seal; jars with a screw band should have the band loosened a quarter of a turn.

Processing the Jars of Vegetables

Put water in the base of the pressure cooker to a depth of about 2 inches and heat until simmering. Place a rack in the cooker and stand the jars on it, making sure that they don't touch each other or the sides of the cooker. Cover the cooker and continue heating until steam comes through the vent; allow this to continue for at least 7 minutes. Bring the cooker up to 10 lb. pressure and maintain it for the necessary time (see table, page 113–4). Remove the cooker from heat and allow it to cool slowly until the pressure is normal again. Remove the lid from the cooker and take out the jars. Tighten the screw bands if used. Put the jars in a warm place and allow them to cool before handling further.

Storing the Sealed jars: see fruit (page 111) but do not re-process badly sealed jars.

Using the Vegetables

Reheat the vegetables in the brine in which they were bottled. If there is any doubt that the vegetables are in good condition, either from smell or appearance, discard them without even tasting. When the bottles are opened there should be no rush of escaping air or gases.

Freezing Fruit and Vegetables

Freezing fruit and vegetables is the best method of preserving them with their original colour, flavour, texture and food value intact. There is little or no deterioration over a period of about 12 months and even after this time it is only slight, if the fruit and vegetables have been prepared and packed carefully initially. The disadvantage of using a freezer for storing fruit and vegetables is that it can take up valuable space in your home and bulky vegetables take up a lot of space in the freezer. Also the running cost of the machine must be taken into account.

If you decide to buy a freezer, it is advisable to go carefully and fully into the various types that are available; check that you have a suitable place to put it and also sufficient space. The size will also be determined by the number of people in your family.

Besides the freezer itself, you will have to buy small containers in which to store the food for freezing. Here also there is a big choice but whichever you choose make sure that they are moisture-proof. Plastic boxes, polythene bags and waxed cartons are all suitable for fruit and vegetables. Special "freezer tape" and plastic or paper-covered wire ties can be used for sealing. It is also a good idea to have some form of labelling as it is sometimes impossible to see just what is in a package when frozen; include the date of freezing, too.

Choosing and Preparing Fruit for Freezing

It is only worth freezing fruit which is just ripe and in its prime. Pick it and freeze it the same day if possible; if there is any delay, store in a cool dark place until you are ready. Only wash the fruit if absolutely necessary and prepare it as you would normally prepare fruit for eating—discard the peel, cores and stones according to the type of fruit. This not only saves space but, in the case of the stones, stops them flavouring the fruit as their flavour intensifies with keeping. Cooked fruit can also be frozen, either puréed, whole, mashed or in pies (with cooked or uncooked pastry). Fruit juices, sweetened or unsweetened, also freeze successfully.

Cooked fruit and fruit juices need to be simply put into moisture-proof containers, leaving ½–1 inch space at the top and placed in the freezer (set at its lowest setting).

Fresh fruit can be frozen by one of the following methods:

(a) **Unsweetened.** Spread the prepared fruit (see above) on trays and place in the freezer for about 12 hours or until well frozen. Pack the frozen fruit into moisture-proof containers.

(b) **Dry Sugar.** Prepare the fruit (see above) and then place it in a bowl. Add 4–6 oz. (about ½–1 cup) castor (superfine) sugar for each pound (2 cups) prepared fruit and mix gently. Pack the fruit into moisture-proof containers leaving about ½ inch space at the top. Delicate fruit such as raspberries and strawberries can be packed in to the containers and layered with the sugar to avoid damaging them. Cover and seal the container and place in the freezer.

(c) **Syrup.** Place 1 pint (2½ cups) water in a saucepan and add 8 oz. (1 cup) to 1 lb. (2 cups) white sugar. Heat gently, stirring until the sugar is dissolved. Remove from the heat and allow to become completely cold before using. Pack the prepared fruit (see above) into moisture-proof containers and pour over enough syrup to cover the fruit but to leave a ½–1 inch space at the top. Cover and seal the container. Place the fruit in the freezer.

Apples are best frozen in slices. Peel, core and cut the apples into ¼–½ inch slices and place them immediately in cold salted water to prevent discolouration. Place the slices in a wire blanching basket (a chip (deep-frying) basket can also be used) and dip them in a saucepan of boiling water to cover for 1 minute. Dip quickly in cold water and then drain thoroughly. Pack the cold blanched apple slices firmly into moisture-proof containers, leaving about ½ inch space at the top.

Sugar need not be added or castor (superfine) sugar—4 oz. ($\frac{2}{3}$ cup) for every lb. prepared apples—can be added between the layers as for method (b) (see page 115).

Apricots need not be peeled but if this is preferred, plunge them into a saucepan of boiling water for 30 seconds then rinse in cold running water and slip the skins off. Cut the fruit in half and remove the stones. Pack and freeze in syrup as for method (c) (see page 115).

Bilberries should be inspected carefully and any blemished berries, stalks (stems) and leaves removed. Wash only if necessary and drain thoroughly. Freeze by any of the 3 methods given on page 115.

Blackberries should be inspected carefully and any damaged or squashy fruit removed. Wash if necessary and drain thoroughly. Freeze by any of the 3 methods given on page 115, but they are especially good when frozen in dry sugar (method b). Use 3–4 oz. (scant $\frac{2}{3}$ cup) castor (superfine) sugar to each pound of blackberries.

Cherries should be washed if necessary drained thoroughly and stoned. They should be frozen in syrup—method c).

Cranberries should be washed if necessary and drained thoroughly. Blemished or squashed fruit, stalks (stems) and leaves should be removed. The berries should then be packed into moisture-proof containers without sugar or syrup and frozen.

Cumquats can be frozen to be used later for making marmalade. Wash them in warm water, dry them and pack whole into polythene bags.

Currants should be carefully inspected for imperfect or squashy fruit, then removed from their stalks. Wash if necessary and drain well. Currants can be frozen by any of the 3 methods given on page 115.

Damsons should be washed if necessary drained well and the stones removed. They should be frozen in syrup, by method (c) (see page 115).

Gooseberries should be carefully inspected and imperfect fruit removed. Top and tail and wash if necessary. Place the gooseberries in a wire basket and immerse them in a saucepan of boiling water for 1 minute. Drain, then rinse in cold running water. Drain again thoroughly. Pack and freeze as for methods (a) or (b) on page 115.
Unblanched clean gooseberries can be successfully frozen in syrup by method (c) (see page 115).

Grapefruit can be very successfully frozen after being peeled and the fruit divided into segments with all the skin removed. Pack and freeze by either method (b) or (c) on page 115.

Loganberries should be inspected carefully and any damaged berries, stalks and leaves removed. They can be packed and frozen by any of the 3 methods given on page 115.

Melon should be prepared by removing the pips (seeds), cutting the flesh off the rind and cutting it into $\frac{1}{2}$–$\frac{1}{4}$ inch cubes. Alternatively the melon can be cut into balls with a special cutter. Pack and freeze the melon as for method (b) on page 115. Use 3–4 oz. (scant $\frac{2}{3}$ cup) castor (superfine) sugar for each pound of melon.

Mulberries should be inspected carefully and any damaged berries, stalks and leaves removed. They can be packed and frozen by any of the 3 methods given on page 115.

Nectarines should be peeled by being plunged into a saucepan of boiling water for 30 seconds. After rinsing in cold running water, you can slip the skins off easily. Cut the fruit in half remove the stones and freeze in syrup by method (c) (see page 115). Work quickly to prevent the fruit becoming discoloured.

Oranges for making marmalade at a later date can be frozen by packing the whole clean fruit in polythene bags. Extra fruit or commercial pectin may have to be added when making the marmalade as there is a loss of about 10%.

Passion Fruit pulp can be successfully frozen. Cut the passion fruit in half, scoop out the pulp directly into a moisture-proof container. Leave $\frac{1}{2}$–1 inch space at the top, seal and freeze.

Peaches should be prepared and frozen by exactly the same method as nectarines.

Pears do not freeze very successfully as the delicate flavour soon becomes lost. If you have a glut, however, try freezing them in syrup by method (c) (on page 115). Peel, core and slice or quarter the fruit. Work quickly to avoid discolouration.

Pineapple freezes well. Select well-ripened fruit, peel and remove the core. Cut the pineapple into $\frac{1}{2}$–$\frac{3}{4}$ inch cubes and freeze in syrup by method (c) (see page 115).

Plums should be washed and dried then cut in half and the stones removed. Pack and freeze in syrup by method (c) (see page 115). Work quickly to avoid the fruit becoming discoloured.

Raspberries should be inspected carefully and damaged fruit, stalks (stems) and leaves discarded. If you suspect that there may be maggots, spread the fruit out on a shallow dish and leave it in a cool place for 1 hour, in which time the maggots will emerge. Only wash the fruit if absolutely necessary, drain well. Freeze by methods (a) or (b) on page 115.

Rhubarb should be trimmed at each end, washed and dried well then cut into $1\frac{1}{2}$–2 inch lengths. Place it in a wire basket and blanch it by plunging it into a saucepan of boiling water for 1 minute then rinsing in cold running water. Freeze by packing the fruit into moisture-proof containers with sugar or syrup, see method (b) or (c) on page 115.

Strawberries should be inspected carefully and damaged berries, hulls and stalks (stems) removed. Only wash if absolutely necessary, drain well. Strawberries can be frozen by any of the 3 methods on page 115, but are most successful by method (a).

Tomatoes can only be frozen when cooked or as juice. Place even-sized tomatoes in a wire basket and plunge them into a saucepan of boiling water for 2 minutes. Cool in cold running water for about 5 minutes. Slip off the skins and pack the tomatoes into moisture-proof containers, leaving about $\frac{1}{2}$ inch space at the top. Seal and freeze. The cooked tomatoes can also be rubbed through a sieve to make a purée. Season lightly with sugar, salt and pepper before packing and freezing as for the whole tomatoes. This can make a delicious tomato cocktail; season with lemon juice and Worcestershire sauce before serving.

Thawing and Using Frozen Fruit

Thaw the fruit in the unopened container. For fruit which discolours easily, turn the container upside down so that the fruit is kept covered in syrup. Defrosting times will vary according to the fruit and the size of the pack. Thaw the fruit either at room temperature or in the refrigerator.

Dessert Fruit. Serve the fruit when it is only just thawed or when there are still a few ice crystals left.

Stewing Fruit. Thaw until the fruit can be separated then cook in its own syrup or put into pies, as desired.

Choosing and Preparing Vegetables for Freezing

Vegetables freeze well if they are carefully prepared. They must be prepared ready for serving then blanched in boiling water. Place a few vegetables at a time (up to 1 lb. prepared weight) in a wire basket and plunge the basket into a large saucepan of rapidly boiling water. Different vegetables must be blanched for different lengths of time; start timing from the moment the water comes back to the boil (this should not be more than a minute after the vegetables have been put in.) The same water can be used for the next batch of vegetables, up to about 8 batches. Shake the wire basket occasionally very gently to move the vegetables and make sure that they are all blanched. Immediately after blanching, place the vegetables (still in the basket) in a bowl under cold running water. Drain very thoroughly before packing into moisture-proof containers, sealing, labelling and finally, freezing.

Prepare the vegetables as given below:

Asparagus should be trimmed then washed in cold water before blanching. Do not tie in bundles. Grade the stalks according to thickness and blanch (see above) thick stalks for 2 minutes, thin stalks for 4 minutes. Rinse in cold water for 4 minutes.

Broad (Lima) Beans should be shelled and only the young small beans frozen. Blanch (as described previously) for 2 minutes then rinse in cold water for 3 minutes.

French and Runner Beans should be washed, then stringed and the ends cut off. Small beans can be frozen whole, otherwise slice them. Blanch (see above) for 2–5 minutes, depending on size and whether they are whole or sliced. Rinse in cold water for 3–5 minutes.

Broccoli should have the stalks trimmed, and all hard woody parts removed. The heads should be graded according to size for blanching. Blanch for 3–5 minutes (see above) then rinse in cold water for 4 minutes.

Brussels Sprouts should be selected carefully and only small tight sprouts used. Remove the outer leaves and blanch (see above) for 3–4 minutes. Rinse in cold water for 5 minutes.

Cabbage should be carefully washed and the leaves trimmed. Freeze either whole or shredded. Blanch (see above) for 1–2 minutes, rinse in cold water for 2–3 minutes. After packing the containers, leave $\frac{1}{2}$–1 inch space at the top.

Carrots for freezing should be young and tender. Either scrape the carrots before blanching, if they are to be sliced, or if they are to be left whole, rub the skins off after blanching. Blanch (see above) for 3–5 minutes, depending on the size and whether they are cut or whole. Rinse in cold water for 4–5 minutes.

Cauliflower should be broken into flowerettes of even size. Blanch (as described) for 3–6 minutes, according to the size of the flowerettes. Rinse in cold water for 3–5 minutes.

Corn can be frozen either on the cob or as separate kernels. Choose very young and tender corn and freeze it as soon as possible after harvesting. Remove the husk and silk and blanch for 5–8 minutes, according to size. Cool in cold water for about 10 minutes and then either freeze whole or scrape the kernels off the cob and freeze them separately.

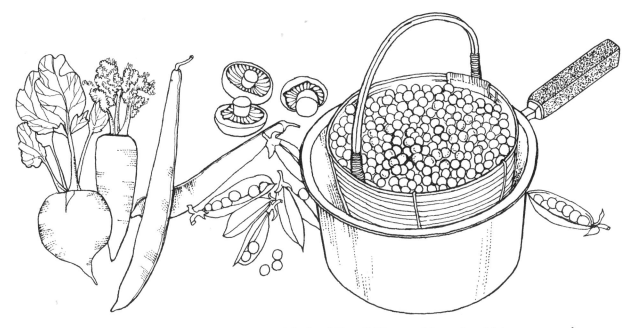

Mushrooms should be washed and dried thoroughly but peeled only if necessary. Do not blanch mushrooms, spread them out onto trays and place them in the freezer overnight. Pack in moisture-proof containers next day and store. Alternatively, fry the mushrooms very gently in a little butter, cool them quickly then pack them into containers and freeze.

Parsnips should be peeled and cut into 1½ inch dice or slices. Blanch, (see page 118) for 1–2 minutes and cool in cold water for 2 minutes.

Peas should be young, tender and freshly picked. Pod (shell) them and sort them carefully. Blanch (see page 118) for 1 minute then cool them in cold water for 2–3 minutes.

Peppers should be washed, cut into halves or quarters and the seeds and membranes removed. Blanch (see page 118) for 2–3 minutes and cool in cold water for 4–5 minutes.

Potatoes can be frozen as new potatoes, chips (French fried) or cooked mashed. New potatoes should be scraped and cooked until almost tender, in the usual way. Cool in cold water then freeze. Chips (French fried) should be prepared in the normal way and fried until they are tender but not yet browned. Cool and freeze. Mashed potatoes can be frozen as ready-prepared Duchesse potatoes, croquettes or on top of such dishes as cottage pie.

Spinach should be cleaned carefully and the mid-rib removed. Blanch a few leaves at a time (see page 118) for 2 minutes. Cool in cold water for 2–3 minutes. When packing the spinach into containers, leave ½–1 inch space at the top.

Swedes should be prepared and frozen as for parsnips.

Mixed Vegetables should be prepared separately according to the individual variety and mixed after cooling and before packing into the containers for freezing.

Ratatouille can be prepared according to your recipe and packed into moisture-proof containers for freezing. Leave ½–1 inch space at the top.

Using Frozen Vegetables

Frozen vegetables should preferably not be thawed before cooking. They can be cooked in the same way as freshly picked vegetables but the cooking must be shortened as they are already partially cooked. Only cook them for a quarter of the normal cooking time. Mushrooms are usually fried in a little butter, without thawing first.

The exception to this rule is corn on the cob. This should be defrosted in the unopened pack before cooking.

Herbs can also be frozen with great success. Parsley can be dipped in boiling water for 5 seconds, then cooled in cold water before freezing to help keep the colour, but this is not entirely necessary. Simply place the herbs, in sprigs, in moisture-proof containers and freeze. Herbs can be chopped very easily when frozen. Frozen parsley cannot be used for garnishing—only as flavouring.

Trouble-shooting with food freezing
Discoloured, dry patches:
(a) The container was not moisture-proof

Unfrozen packs:
(a) The freezer is not working. This may be due to a power failure, fuse blown or faulty appliance. Discard the pack.

Drying Fruit, Vegetables and Herbs

Home drying of fruit, vegetables and herbs is not as popular as it used to be, which is a pity as it has some advantages over the other methods of preserving. No expensive equipment is needed; the process is simple and requires no critical timing although temperature can be vital; storage is simple and takes up very little space.

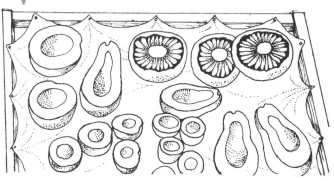

Drying can be done out of doors and this is the usual way in those parts of the world that are blessed with a balmy, sunny climate. For outside drying, it is advisable to make "trays", using a frame of 4 slats of wood, with muslin stretched across the middle. The prepared fruit and vegetables are spread on to the muslin and then placed on a table in the sun until dry. This can take a little time, so take the trays in at night and put them out in the sun again next morning. It is a good idea to place another piece of muslin over the loaded trays to prevent dust and insects from getting to the fruit and vegetables.

Those of us who cannot use the sun for drying can very successfully use artificial heat. The plate rack over the cooker, the residual heat in the oven after cooking and an airing cupboard with a hot water tank in it are all suitable. It is a good idea to invest in a thermometer to check that the heat is not too high. There is also a need for good air circulation, so leave the oven door ajar or the airing cupboard door slightly open if you are using these places. As with outdoor drying, the produce is spread on trays. For small amounts such as might be dried in the oven, try spreading the actual oven shelf with muslin.

Choosing and Preparing Fruit

Use perfect, just-ripe fruit. Under-ripe and over-ripe fruit does not compare favourably in flavour or colour with the just-ripe fruit when dried. The prepared fruit (see below) is spread on to the trays and heated very gently. Initially the heat should be about 120°F (50°C) and then increased until it is about 140°F (60°C). Overheating at first tends to harden the outside of the fruit; the final temperature should never exceed 150°F (65°C).

Apples are usually dried in rings. Peel, core and slice the apples into ¼ inch thick slices. Place the prepared rings into salt water (1 oz. salt to 4 pints (10 cups) cold water) for a few minutes to prevent discolouration. Either spread the rings on to trays or thread them onto thin sticks or skewers and dry them suspended in this way. Never allow the temperature to exceed 140°F (60°C) and the whole process will take about 6 hours. The drying time can be spread over 2 or 3 days if the heating is not continuous. Allow the rings to stand in a cool, dark place for 12 hours before storing. Dried apples are spongy, they resemble chamois leather in texture.

Apricots are usually dried in halves. Remove the stones and spread the fruit onto the trays. Heat for 2 hours at a temperature of 130°F (55°C), then remove from the heat and leave until next day. Continue heating at a temperature not exceeding 150°F (65°C) until dry. Dried apricots are not brittle but should be springy; no juice should appear when the fruit is cut. Allow the apricots to stand in a cool, dark place for 12 hours before storing.

Peaches can be dried as for apricots. Choose a brightly coloured variety.

Pears are dried either in quarters or halves, as for apple rings.

Plums are dried as for apricots. The initial temperature however should be lower and not exceed 120°F (50°C) or the skins may split.

The fruits mentioned above dry better than most others. Small soft fruit and berries become small, hard and shrivelled and do not regain their original appearance after soaking.

Choosing and Preparing Vegetables
Beans: runner (snap) beans, French (string) beans and broad (Lima) beans can all be dried. Large runner (snap) beans should be sliced, all other beans dried whole. Place them in a wire basket and immerse it in boiling water for 2–5 minutes according to the age of the beans. The drained beans are then spread onto trays and placed in a temperature of 120°F, (50°C). This is gradually increased to 150°F (65°C). The dried beans should be crisp. Cool before storing.

Mushrooms dry well but should be very fresh initially. Peel the mushrooms if necessary and remove the stalks. Thread onto thin string or spread them on to trays. Dry the prepared mushrooms in a temperature not exceeding 120°F (50°C) until they are crisp. Cool before storing.

Onions can be tricky to dry as they scorch and shrivel if care is not taken. Cut them into thin slices and blanch them in boiling water for 1 minute. Spread the slices on trays and dry as for mushrooms.

These vegetables are the best and most rewarding ones to dry. Root vegetables can usually be stored without drying. A mixture of vegetables however can be useful for soups and stews. Cut the selected vegetables (carrots, parsnips, potatoes, leeks, celery) into dice. Blanch them in boiling water for 2–3 minutes, drain and dry in a temperature not exceeding 150°F (65°C). The finished vegetables should be crisp.

Choosing and Preparing Herbs
All herbs are suitable for drying. They should be picked before they flower and early in the morning, when they are dry but not warmed by the sun.

Small-leaved herbs such as sage, thyme, mar-joram, rosemary, can be simply dried by hanging in bunches in a warm place. This can be out of doors, in an airing cupboard (warming oven) or over the cooker. The bunch should be protected against dust and insects by a muslin bag or even a brown paper bag.

Large-leaved herbs such as mint or bay, can also be dried in the open air but a better result is obtained if they are dried more quickly. The leaves should be picked from the stems then tied loosely in a muslin bag and plunged into a saucepan of boiling water for 1 minute. Drain the leaves and then spread them on trays and dry at a temperature of about 120°F (50°C) until crisp. This will take about 1 hour.

Parsley is the exception when drying. Tie the parsley into a loose bunch and dip it into a saucepan of boiling water for 1 minute. Drain off the excess moisture then place the bunch in a hot oven (400°F Mark 6) for 1 minute. Turn the oven off, open the door and allow the parsley to dry in the residual heat.

Storing Dried Fruit, Vegetables and Herbs
It is not wise to store dried fruit in an airtight container. It is best kept in cardboard, plastic or wooden boxes that are not entirely airtight. Vegetables, however, should be sealed airtight. Herbs are usually crushed and stored in small screw-top jars or tins. All three should be kept in a cool and dark place.

Using Dried Fruit, Vegetables and Herbs
Fruit and vegetables need to be soaked for a time before they are cooked. Soak fruit for 24–48 hours, in plenty of water. Soak vegetables for 12–24 hours, in plenty of water. Cook the fruit or vegetables in a little of the water used for soaking. Add the sugar to the fruit after the cooking time is completed.
Herbs can be added directly to the dish that they are to flavour. A good tip to remember is that 1 tablespoon (1¼T) chopped fresh herbs is equal to 1 teaspoon crushed dried herbs.

Trouble-shooting with drying fruit, vegetables and herbs

Fruit mouldy or musty after storage:
(a) The container was sealed airtight.
(b) The storage place was damp.

Vegetables soft or slimy after storage:
(a) The container was not airtight.
(b) The storage place was damp.

Herbs with poor colour and flavour:
(a) They were not at their best when picked.
(b) They were overheated.

Overleaf: Dried Apple Rings

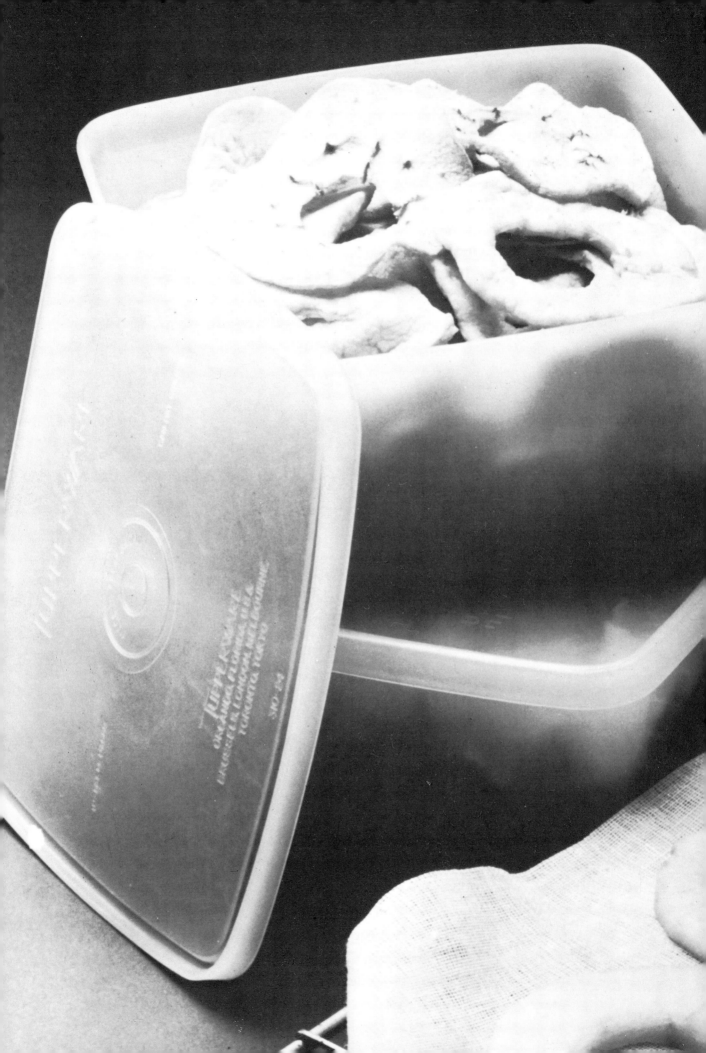

Salting Vegetables and Curing Hams and Bacon

Beans are usually the only vegetables which are stored by salting and even they are more acceptable to modern palates when preserved by other means. The process however is very simple and worth trying if you are faced with a glut of French (string) or runner (snap) beans.
Before the days of freezing and refrigeration, keeping meat was a great problem. When an animal was killed the meat either had to be given away or sold to local people to be eaten promptly or it went bad. Pork was especially hazardous to keep and soon pickling and curing of pork became general and, in Britain, different regions developed their own methods of curing.

Wash the beans and slice them if they are large. Small beans can be left whole. Use 1 lb. cooking salt for each 3 lb. beans. Place a $\frac{1}{2}$ inch layer of the salt in the bottom of a large earthenware or glass jar, reserve an equal amount for the top and mix the remainder with the beans. Place the salt and beans in the jar, packing them firmly. Finish with a $\frac{1}{2}$ inch layer of salt on the top. Cover the jar and put aside for 2–3 days. Add more beans to the jar as necessary, finishing each time with $\frac{1}{2}$ inch layer of salt on the top. Cover the jar with a moisture-proof cover and place it in a cool place for storage.

To use the beans, wash them in several changes of water then soak them in warm water for 2 hours. Cook in a saucepan of boiling unsalted water for about 20 minutes or until tender.

Sauerkraut

Sauerkraut is, strictly speaking, salted cabbage. Unlike salted beans, however, it is essential that it is fermented to obtain the desired result.

5 lb. cabbage (prepared)
2 oz. cooking salt

Prepare the cabbage by discarding the outer leaves and the core. Shred the heart (head) finely.
Place the cabbage in a bowl, add the salt and mix thoroughly. Pack into a large jar (wood is ideal but earthenware, glass or china can also be used). Place a saucer or plate on top of the cabbage and put heavy weights on top. The plate should cover the cabbage entirely. Put the jar aside for 2–3 weeks in a warm place (about 75°F). After a few days the plate should be covered with brine; remove the scum which will rise to the surface, every 2–3 days. If the plate is not covered with brine after the first few days and at any subsequent time, add more brine (made by dissolving about 1 tablespoon ($1\frac{1}{4}$T) salt in 1 pint ($2\frac{1}{2}$ cups) water.

The sauerkraut may now be used. The extra not used immediately can be preserved by draining off the brine into a large saucepan, bringing it to the boil then adding the cabbage and returning it to simmering. Pack the hot sauerkraut into hot clean jars, cover and stand the jars in a saucepan with a false bottom. Cover with boiling water and process for 25 minutes. Seal the jars tightly and cool.

Curing Hams and Bacon

The basic pickling and curing operation is nearly always the same wherever it is carried out. Some of the ingredients are not too readily available but if you shop around they certainly can be found.

Ask your butcher to cut up the pig into joints as you require them or try just one joint to start with. A piece of belly pork would be an economical cut to try; it makes a delicious and inexpensive meal as pickled pork or, when thinly sliced, makes streaky bacon.

Prepare a strong brine by placing 2 lb. bay salt

Salting Beans

(rock salt can also be used), 2 lb. cooking salt, 1¼ oz. saltpetre in a saucepan with 1½ gallons (30 cups) water. Bring to the boil, making sure that the salt and saltpetre are thoroughly dissolved. Strain if necessary. Allow the brine to cool then place the pork in a large bowl and pour the brine over. If the pork is to be eaten as pickled pork, leave it immersed for 24 hours then dry it before storing it in a cool place. If you are making ham, leave the pork in the brine just long enough to clean it—about 10 minutes for small joints and up to 1 hour for large hams. Press the meat to remove any blood. Drain the meat.

Plain Cure	Sweet Cure
10 lb. pork	10 lb. pork
1 lb. salt	1 lb. salt
½ oz. saltpetre	½ oz. saltpetre
	6 oz. (1 cup) soft brown sugar or 8 oz. (1 cup) treacle (molasses)

NOTE: Additional flavourings can be added either to the plain or sweet cure. Some you could try are: crushed juniper berries; ground cloves; ground coriander; ground black pepper.

Weigh the pork and allow for each 10 lb. the ingredients given above. Mix the curing ingredients together and rub them all over the pork.

The pork must now be covered completely in extra salt. Place a 1–2 inch layer in the bottom of a container, place the meat on top, pack more salt around the sides then finish with a 1–2 inch layer on top of the meat. Put aside in a cool place for 5 days.

Sprinkle more of the curing mixture onto the meat and repack it in salt. Put aside again in a cool place for 2–5 weeks according to the size of the joint.

Scrape any salt off the meat and wash it with a cloth wrung out in hot water. Dry the meat. Tie a piece of string around the pork and hang it to dry thoroughly in a warm, light airy place. (This will take 1–3 weeks).

Wrap the dried joint in greaseproof (waxed) paper and then place in a calico bag and hang it in a cool dry place.

Smoking the ham is the most tricky process. There are various short cuts such as using ingredients which impart a "smoky" flavour (such as a special salt or a liquid which can be painted on). Alternatively, a fire can be made of smouldering oak or ash sawdust and the smoke trapped in a container such as a wooden barrel or a dustbin. The ham is hung in the smoky atmosphere and a damp sack is placed over the top. The temperature should never exceed 90°F. Smoke for 3 days.

Store the ham as for unsmoked hams, wrapped in greaseproof (waxed) paper and calico and hung in a cool dry place.

Index

Figures in italics refer to illustrations.

Almond:
  Apple and almond jam 16
  Pear and almond jam 32
Apple:
  To bottle apples 99, 107, 108
  To dry apples 120, *122*
  To freeze apples 115
  Apple and almond jam 16
  Apple and banana chutney 86
  Apple chutney 85
  Apple cinnamon jelly 17
  Apple and date chutney 86
  Apple clove jam 16
  Apple clove jelly 17
  Apple and date chutney 86
  Apple geranium jelly 17
  Apple ginger butter 61
  Apple ginger jam 16
  Apple ginger jelly 17
  Apple ginger preserve 17
  Apple jelly 17
  Apple juice 65
  Apple lemon jelly 17
  Apple mint jelly 17
  Apple orange preserve 17
  Apple and pear chutney 86
  Apple and pear jam 16
  Apple peppermint jelly 17
  Apple preserve 17, *105*
  Apple and red pepper chutney 86
  Apple and tomato chutney 87
  Apricot and apple jam 18
  Blackberry and apple jam 19
  Blackberry and apple jelly 20
  Black currant and apple jam 22
  Dried apricot, apple and cider jam 18
  Elderberry and apple jelly 24
  Fig and apple jam 26, *44*
  Mulberry and apple jam 31
  Pickled apples 81
  Pineapple in apple jelly 17, *28*
  Plum and apple jam 35
  Sharp apple chutney 86
  Spiced apple butter 61
  Strawberry and apple jam 43
  Sweet pickle and apple 81
  Tomato, apple and raisin chutney 95
Apricot:
  To bottle apricots 99, *102*, 107, 108
  To dry apricots 120
  To freeze apricots 116
  Apricot and apple jam 18
  Apricot butter 61
  Apricot and date chutney 87
  Apricot jam 18, *24*

Apricot rum jam 18
Brandied apricots 67
Dried apricot, apple and cider jam 18
Dried apricot chutney 87
Dried apricot jam 18
Fresh apricot and passion fruit jam 18
Pear and apricot jam 32
Asparagus:
  To bottle asparagus 113, *110*, *111*
  To freeze asparagus 118
Aubergine and pepper relish 88

Banana:
  To Bottle bananas 99, 107, 108
  Apple and banana chutney 86
  Banana jam 18
Beans, Broad (Lima), French (String) and Runner (Snap):
  To bottle beans 113
  To dry beans 121
  To freeze beans 118
  To salt beans 124, *125*
Beetroot:
  To bottle beetroot 113
  Beetroot and onion pickle 74
  Beetroot pickle 74
  Sweet beetroot pickle 74
Bengal chutney 88
Bilberry:
  To bottle bilberries 99, 107, 108
  To freeze bilberries 116
Blackberry:
  To bottle blackberries 99, 107, 108
  To freeze blackberries 117
  Blackberry and apple jam 19
  Blackberry and apple jelly 20
  Blackberry and elderberry jam 19
  Blackberry jam 18
  Blackberry jelly 20
  Blackberry and marrow jam 19
  Blackberry sauce 98
  Spiced blackberry jelly 20
Black currant:
  Bottled black currents 100, 107, 108
  Black currant and apple jam 22
  Black currant jam 20
  Black currant jelly 23
  Rhubarb and black currant jelly 39
Bottling fruit 99–111:
  Choosing and preparing the jars 104
  Filling the jars 106
  Processing the jars of fruit 106–9
  Storing the sealed jars 111
  Syrup for bottling 103–4
  Trouble-shooting with bottled fruit 111
  Using the bottled fruit 111
Bottling vegetables:

Choosing, preparing and filling the jars 114
Choosing and preparing the vegetables 111–14
Making the brine 114
Processing the jars of vegetables 114
Storing the sealed jars 114
Brandied apricots 67
Brandied cherries 67
Brandied cumquats 67
Brandied four fruit jam 47
Brandied grapes 67
Brandied orange marmalade 52
Brandied peaches 67, *70*
Brine 114
Broccoli:
  To bottle broccoli 113
  To freeze broccoli 118
Brussels sprouts:
  To bottle brussels sprouts 113
  To freeze brussels sprouts 118

Cabbage:
  To freeze cabbage 118
  Sauerkraut 124
Candied fruits 67–70, *71*
Carrot:
  To bottle carrots 113
  To freeze carrots 118
Cauliflower:
  To bottle cauliflower 113
  To freeze cauliflower 118
  Cauliflower pickle 74
  Sweet cauliflower pickle 76
Celery:
  To bottle celery 113
  Celery vinegar 73
  Sweet celery and tomato chutney 88
Cherry:
  To bottle cherries 99, 107, 108
  To freeze cherries 117
  Black cherry preserve 23
  Brandied cherries 67
  Cherry conserve 22
  Cherry jam 22
  Cherry and orange jam 22
  Cherry preserve 22
  Pickled cherries 76
  Spiced cherry jam 22
Chilli vinegar 72, *73*
Chinese gooseberry:
  To bottle Chinese gooseberries 99, 107, 108
  Chinese gooseberry and grapefruit jam 23
Choko chutney 92
Chutneys:
  Cooking and completing chutneys 85
  Trouble-shooting with chutneys 85
  recipes:
  Apple and banana chutney 86
  Apple chutney 85
  Apple and date chutney 86
  Apple and pear chutney 86
  Apple and red pepper chutney 86

Apple and tomato chutney 87
Apricot and date chutney 87
Bengal chutney 88
Choko chutney 92
Dried apricot chutney 87
Gooseberry chutney 91, *92*
Green tomato chutney 95
Lemon chutney 91, *89*
Mango chutney 92
Marrow chutney 92
Orange chutney 91
Pear and ginger chutney 93, *97*
Plum chutney 93
Rhubarb chutney 93
Ripe tomato chutney 95
Sharp apple chutney 86
Sweet celery and tomato chutney 88
Tomato, apple and raisin chutney 95
Tomato and marrow chutney 95
Cinnamon apple jelly 17
Cinnamon plum jam 35
Corn-on-the-cob:
  To bottle corn 113
  To freeze corn 118
  Corn and pear relish 90
  Corn relish 88
Courgette (Zucchini):
  To bottle courgettes 113
  Pickled courgettes 76
Crab apple:
  To bottle crab apple 99
  Pickled crab apples 81
Cranberry:
  To bottle cranberries 99
  To freeze cranberries 117
  Cranberry jam 23
Cucumber:
  Cucumber and tomato relish 90
  Cucumber vinegar 73
  Pickled cucumber 76
  Sweet cucumber pickle 76
Curing hams and pork 124–5
Cumquat:
  To bottle cumquats 100, 108
  To freeze cumquats 117
  Brandied cumquats 67
  Cumquat marmalade 53
Currant. *See also* Black and red currants
  To bottle currants 100, 107, 108
  To freeze currants 117
  Currant jelly 23
  Currant and raspberry jelly 23
  Gooseberry and currant jelly 26

Damson:
  To bottle damsons 100, 107, 108
  To freeze damsons 117
  Damson cheese 61
  Damson jam 24
  Damson jelly 24
Date:
  Apple and date chutney 86

Apricot and date chutney 87

Egg:
  Pickled eggs 81
Eggplant *see* Aubergine
Elderberry:
  Blackberry and elderberry jam, 19
  Elderberry and apple jelly 24
  Elderberry jelly 24
  Gooseberry and elderberry jam 26

Fig:
  To bottle figs 100, 107, 108
  Dried fig jam 25
  Fig and apple jam 26, *44*
  Fresh fig jam 25
Freezing fruit 115–18
Freezing vegetables 118–19
Fruit. *See also* Apple, Apricot etc.
  To choose and cook fruit for jams 11, *21*
  To find pectin content of fruit 11
  To strain fruit for jelly 11, *12*
  Bottled fruits 99–111, *101*
  Brandied four fruit jam 47
  Candied fruits 67–70, *70–1*
  Dried fruit 120
  Freezing fruit 115–18
  Fresh fruit jam 47, 49
  Fruit butters 58
  Fruit cheeses 58
  Fruit curds and honey 58
  Fruit juices 65, 66
  Fruit pastes 58
  Fruit pulp or purée 103
  Fruit syrup 64
  Fruit vinegars 73
  Mixed tropical fruit jam 47
  Three fruit jelly marmalade 53
  Three fruit marmalade 52

Gherkin:
  Pickled gherkins 76
Ginger:
  Apple ginger butter 61
  Apple ginger jam 16
  Apple ginger jelly 17
  Apple ginger preserve 17
  Lemon ginger marmalade 49
  Marrow and ginger jam 30
  Pear and ginger chutney 93, *97*
  Pear and ginger jam 32
  Pear and ginger preserve 32, *33*
  Rhubarb and ginger jam 38
Gooseberry:
  To bottle gooseberries 100, 107, 108
  To freeze gooseberries 117
  Gooseberry cheese 61
  Gooseberry chutney 91, *92*

Gooseberry and currant jelly 26
Gooseberry and elderberry jam 26
Gooseberry jam 26
Gooseberry jelly 26
Gooseberry and red currant jam 26
Strawberry and gooseberry jam 43
Strawberry and gooseberry jelly 43
Grape:
  To bottle grapes 102
  Brandied grapes 67
  Grape cheese 61
  Grape jam 26
  Grape jelly 27
  Grape and orange jam 27
  Pickled grapes 81
  Spiced grape jelly 27
Grapefruit:
  To bottle grapefruit 102, 107, 108
  To freeze grapefruit 117
  Chinese gooseberry and grapefruit jam 23
  Grapefruit curd 62
  Grapefruit jelly marmalade 53
  Grapefruit and lemon marmalade 52
  Grapefruit marmalade 52
Green tomato chutney 95
Green tomato pickle 80
Green tomato sauce 96
Greengage jam 27
Guava jelly 26

Hams, to cure 125
Herbs:
  To dry herbs 121
  To freeze herbs 119
  Herbed vinegar 72
Honeyed strawberry jam 43
Horseradish sauce 98

Jams, Jellies and marmalades. *(See also under individual fruits)*
  Adding the sugar 12
  Choosing the fruit 11
  Completing the jam 15
  Cooking the fruit 11
  Covering and storing jars 15, *46*
  Flake test 14
  Straining fruit for jelly 11
  Sugarless jam 49
  Temperature test 14
  Testing for setting point 12
  Trouble-shooting with jams etc. 15–16
  Volume test 12
  Weight test 12
  Wrinkle test 14
Japonica jam 27
Japonica jam, spiced 27
Jellies *see* Jams, Jellies and marmalades

Ketchups *see* Sauces and ketchups

Leek:
  To bottle leeks 113

Lemon:
  To bottle lemons 102, 107, 108
  Apple lemon jelly 17
  Grapefruit and lemon marmalade 52
  Lemon chutney 91, *89*
  Lemon curd 61, *59, 63*
  Lemon ginger marmalade 49
  Lemon marmalade 49
  Lemon squash 65
  Marrow and lemon jam 30
  Spiced lemon marmalade 49
Loganberry:
  To freeze loganberries 117
  Loganberry jam 27
  Loganberry jelly 27

Mango chutney 92
Marmalade:
  Brandied orange marmalade 52
  Chunky dark marmalade 52
  Cumquat marmalade 53
  Grapefruit jelly marmalade 53
  Grapefruit and lemon marmalade 52
  Grapefruit marmalade 52
  Orange coriander marmalade 52
  Orange jelly marmalade 53
  Seville orange marmalade 49
  Sweet orange marmalade 52
  Tangerine marmalade 52
  Three fruit jelly marmalade 53
  Three fruit marmalade 52
Marrow (Marrow squash):
  Blackberry and marrow jam 19
  Marrow chutney 92
  Marrow conserve 30
  Marrow and ginger jam 30
  Marrow and lemon jam 30
  Tomato and marrow chutney 95
Melon:
  To freeze melons 117
  Melon conserve 30
Mincemeat 62, *63*
Mint:
  Apple mint jelly 17
  Mint jelly 30
  Mint relish 93
  Mint sauce 98
Mixed tropical fruit jam 47
Mulberry:
  To bottle mulberries 102, 107, 108
  To freeze mulberries 117
  Mulberry and apple jam 31
  Mulberry jam 30
  Seedless mulberry jam 31
Mushroom:
  To bottle mushrooms 113–14
  To dry mushrooms 121
  To freeze mushrooms 119
  Mushroom ketchup 96
  Pickled mushrooms 77

Nectarine:
  To bottle nectarines 102, 107, 108
  To freeze nectarines 117

Onion:
  To dry onions 121
  Beetroot and onion pickle 74
  Onion vinegar 73
  Pickled onions 77, *77*
Orange:
  To bottle oranges 102, 107, 108
  To freeze oranges 117
  Apple orange preserve 17
  Cherry and orange jam 22
  Brandied orange marmalade 52
  Chunky dark marmalade 52
  Grape and orange jam 27
  Orange chutney 92
  Orange coriander marmalade 52
  Orange curd 62
  Orange jelly marmalade 53
  Orange squash 65
  Rhubarb and orange butter 58
  Rhubarb and orange jam 38
  Rhubarb and orange jelly 39
  Seville orange marmalade 49
  Spiced orange slices 82, *79*
  Sweet orange marmalade 52

Parsley, to dry 121
Parsnip, to freeze 119
Passion fruit:
  To bottle passion fruit 102, 107, 108
  To freeze passion fruit 117
  Fresh apricot and passion fruit jam 18
  Passion fruit honey 62
  Passion fruit jam 31
Pea:
  To bottle peas 114
  To freeze peas 119
Peach:
  To bottle peaches 102, 107, 108
  To dry peaches 121
  To freeze peaches 117
  Brandied peaches 67, *70*
  Dried peach jam 32
  Peach cheese 61
  Peach jam 32
  Peach and pear jam 32
  Pickled peaches 82
Pear:
  To bottle pears 102, 107, 108
  To dry pears 121
  To freeze pears 117
  Apple and pear chutney 86
  Apple and pear jam 16
  Corn and pear relish 90
  Peach and pear jam 32
  Pear and almond jam 32
  Pear and apricot jam 32
  Pear clove jam 32

Pear conserve 30
Pear and ginger chutney 93, 97
Pear and ginger jam 32
Pear and ginger preserve 32, 33
Pear jam 32
Pickled pears 82, 103
Pectin 11; commercial 12
Peppers, red and green:
  To bottle peppers 114
  To freeze peppers 119
  Apple and red pepper chutney 86
  Aubergine and pepper relish 88
  Red pepper jelly 93
Piccalilli 80
Pickles 74–82:
  Choosing and preparing vegetables and fruit 74
  Completing the process 74
  Covering and storing the jars 74
  Trouble-shooting with pickles 74
  recipes:
  Beetroot and onion pickle 74
  Beetroot pickle 74
  Cauliflower pickle 74
  Clear mixed pickle 81
  Green tomato pickle 80
  Mixed vegetable pickle 80
  Piccalilli 80
  Pickled apples 81
  Pickled cherries 76
  Pickled courgettes 76
  Pickled crab apples 81
  Pickled cucumber 76
  Pickled eggs 81
  Pickled gherkins 76
  Pickled grapes 81
  Pickled mushrooms 77
  Pickled onions 77
  Pickled peaches 82
  Pickled pears 82
  Pickled plums 82
  Pickled red cabbage 77
  Pickled walnuts 81
  Spiced orange slices 82
  Sweet cucumber pickle 76
  Sweet pickle and apple 81
  Sweet pickled green tomatoes 77
  Sweet walnut pickle 81
Pineapple:
  To bottle pineapples 102, 107, 108
  To freeze pineapples 117
  Pineapple in apple jelly 17, 28
  Pineapple conserve 35

Pineapple jam 35
Plum:
  To bottle plums 102, 107, 108
  To dry plums 121
  To freeze plums 117
  Cinnamon plum jam 35
  Pickled plums 82
  Plum and apple jam 35
  Plum chutney 93
  Plum gumbo 58
  Plum jam 35
  Plum sauce 98
Pork, to cure 124–5
Potato:
  To bottle potatoes 114
  To freeze potatoes 119

Quince:
  To bottle quinces 102
  Quince jam 35
  Quince jelly 35

Raspberry:
  To bottle raspberries 102, 107, 108
  To freeze raspberries 117
  Currant and raspberry jelly 23
  Fresh raspberry jam 49
  Raspberry conserve 37
  Raspberry jam 38, 48
  Raspberry jelly 36, 38
  Raspberry and red currant jam 38
  Raspberry and red currant jelly 38
  Rhubarb and raspberry jam 38
  Seedless raspberry jam 38
  Special raspberry jam 38
Ratatouille, to freeze 119
Red cabbage:
  Pickled red cabbage 77
Red currant:
  To bottle redcurrants 100, 107, 108
  Fresh red currant jam 49
  Gooseberry and red currant jam 26
  Raspberry and red currant jam 38
  Raspberry and red currant jelly 38
  Red currant jelly 23, 40, 48
  Strawberry and red currant jelly 47
Relishes:
  Aubergine and pepper relish 88
  Corn and pear relish 90
  Corn relish 88

Cucumber and tomato relish 90
Mint relish 93
Tomato relish 95, 97
Rhubarb:
  To bottle rhubarb 103, 107, 108
  To freeze rhubarb 117
  Rhubarb and black currant jelly 39
  Rhubarb chutney 93
  Rhubarb and ginger jam 38
  Rhubarb jam 37, 38
  Rhubarb and orange butter 58
  Rhubarb and orange jam 38
  Rhubarb and orange jelly 39
  Rhubarb and raspberry jam 38
Rose hip jelly 40
Rose hip jelly, spiced 41
Rose hip syrup 64

Sauces and ketchups:
  Blackberry sauce 98
  Green tomato sauce 96
  Horseradish sauce 98
  Mint sauce 98
  Mushroom ketchup 96
  Plum sauce 98
  Tomato ketchup 96
  Tomato sauce 96
Sauerkraut 124
Seville orange marmalade 49
Spiced apple butter 61
Spiced blackberry jelly 20
Spiced cherry jam 22
Spiced grape jelly 27
Spiced japonica jam 27
Spiced lemon marmalade 49
Spiced orange slices 79, 82
Spiced rose hip jelly 41
Spiced vinegar 72
Spinach, to freeze 119
Strawberry:
  To bottle strawberries 103, 107, 108
  To freeze strawberries 118
  Honeyed strawberry jam 43
  Strawberry and apple jam 43
  Strawberry conserve 43
  Strawberry and gooseberry jam 43
  Strawberry and gooseberry jelly 43
  Strawberry jam 13, 34, 42
  Strawberry and red currant jelly 47

Wholefruit strawberry jam 42
Sugarless jam 49
Swede, to freeze 119
Sweet beetroot pickle 74
Sweet cauliflower pickle 76
Sweet celery and tomato chutney 88
Sweet cucumber pickle 76
Sweet orange marmalade 52
Sweet pickle and apple 81
Sweet pickled green tomatoes 77
Sweet walnut pickle 81
Syrup for bottling 103–4 ..
Syrup for freezing fruit 115

Tangerine curd 62
Tangerine marmalade 62
Three fruit jelly marmalade 53
Three fruit marmalade 52
Tomato:
  To bottle tomatoes 103
  To freeze tomatoes 118
  Apple and tomato chutney 87
  Cucumber and tomato relish 90
  Green tomato chutney 95
  Green tomato pickle 80
  Green tomato sauce 96
  Ripe tomato chutney 95
  Sweet celery and tomato chutney 88
  Sweet pickled green tomatoes 77
  Tomato, apple and raisin chutney 95
  Tomato ketchup 96
  Tomato and marrow chutney 95
  Tomato relish 95, 97
  Tomato sauce 96

Vegetable:
  To bottle vegetables 111–14
  To dry vegetables 121
  To freeze vegetables 118–19
  To salt vegetables 124
  Clear mixed pickle 81
  Mixed vegetable pickle 80
Vinegars 72–3

Walnut:
  Pickled walnuts 81
  Sweet walnut pickle 81
White currant:
  Bottled white currants 100
  White currant jelly 23
Zucchini see Courgette

Acknowledgements

The following colour photographs are by courtesy of:
Angel Studio p. 6, p. 14–15, p. 33, p. 44–45, p. 97, p. 104–5; Conway Picture Library p. 40–41, p. 75, p. 78, p. 79 (below left); John Lee p. 2–3, p. 66 (below), p. 70 (left), p. 70–71, p. 79 (below right); Paf International p. 36, p. 37; Syndication International p. 10, p. 66 (above), p. 79 (above), p. 100, p. 101, p. 109 (above), p. 112; Tupperware p. 48

The following black and white photographs are by courtesy of:
Angel Studio p. 28–29, p. 94; British Farm Produce Council p. 12 (top left & top right), p. 42, p. 56; Certo p. 13, p. 12 (below), p. 34; Conway Picture Library p. 20–21, p. 46–47, p. 50–51, p. 54, p. 55, p. 77, p. 90–91, p. 102, p. 103; H. J. Heinz Co. Ltd. p. 92; Jobling Housecraft Service p. 16; Kilner Jars by Ravenhead p. 110–111; Michael Leale p. 57, p. 60; John Lee p. 63, p. 83; Paf International p. 73; Syndication International p. 24–25, p. 84, p. 125; Tupperware p. 122–123; Tabasco Pepper Sauce p. 89